Abraham Lincoln:

A Spiritual Scientific Portrait

LUIGI MORELLI

ABRAHAM LINCOLN: A SPIRITUAL SCIENTIFIC PORTRAIT

iUniverse books may be ordered through booksellers or by contacting:

iUniverse
1663 Liberty Drive
Bloomington, IN 47403
www.iuniverse.com
844-349-9409

ISBN: 978-1-6632-2641-9 (sc)
ISBN: 978-1-6632-2642-6 (e)

Print information available on the last page.

iUniverse rev. date: 07/19/2021

Contents

Introduction

THIS BOOK IS THE CONTINUATION of work I have done in portraying turning points of the American Revolution, particularly in the figures of Benjamin Franklin and George Washington. In that first attempt I had endeavored to show the symptomatic nature of a great national turning point in the images of the two founders. In this book I will return to the two individuals from an anthroposophical perspective to identify their initiate dimension, and show the guiding hand of fate in the birth of the nation. In a sense I can add here what I could not have said in a book written for the general public.

From an anthroposophical perspective, national icons like Lincoln appear on the scene of history when much is at stake for the future of a nation and of earth evolution. In that sense too there is no mistaking Lincoln's stature. He was that providential individual who tilted the balance of history by being born at the right time and coming to the presidency at the critical moment in which things might have changed for the worse in most imaginable instances.

Individuals of the stature of Lincoln represent an insurmountable obstacle for a historian who follows preestablished views, e.g., a Marxist, a revisionist, or a nationalistic historian, who would judge the man in relation to set parameters or outcomes. Yet one who relies on a purely phenomenological and symptomatic approach to history still has a number of obstacles to overcome. Lincoln is not a man who can be judged from one's store of experience. He cannot be understood other than after an extensive approach, after seeing facet after facet of his personality. Each facet of the personality adds a piece of the puzzle. Once the facets are seen, they need to be reassembled to offer us a feeling for the whole human being. And the whole then appears as the one who embodies the values of the nation and also livingly understands them and penetrates them through his choices and the events of his biography.

There is something fascinating with the hindsight of history in recovering Lincoln's place in America. Here is someone so quintessentially American, one who represents so many of the foundational values and key experiences of being American in the nineteenth century. And here is one who, countering all the obstacles of a modest social extraction and education, nevertheless reaches to all the expectations that presidents before him had fulfilled; he indeed outshines them. Stephen B. Oates mentions that in polls in *Life* magazine (1948), the *New York Times Magazine* (1962), and the *Chicago Tribune Magazine* (1982), scholars and historians consistently ranked Lincoln as the best president in American history.[1] What is it that holds them under this spell?

Looking at Lincoln's life and deeds, as it would be in relation to many other personalities of his stature, is like reading a legend or an engrossing epic novel. From the beginning and up to the very last pages, the odds are stacked against the happy epilogue. Our hero comes from an unlikely position and realizes the forces that oppose him. He tries almost without hope, but moved by an inner, unshakeable conviction that it is at least worth trying. When all is said and done, the hero can look back and see, not just how unlikely the set-up was, but also all those connections, fortuitous events, seeming coincidences, and synchronicities without which nothing would indeed have happened. Such is the experience of looking back at the fate of the United States under the guidance of Lincoln. Under this light we could almost add that not just Lincoln but the nation itself continuously stood on the brink of the abyss waiting to be rescued from some unlikely quarter.

The measure of a man can be revealed by the circumstances in which only his stature could have altered the balance of events. Even, or especially under the harsh conditions of a civil war, an American president in the nineteenth century, for all his power, was only one among many players. He had to contend with others competing for his position and be reelected in the worst possible circumstances; with the members of a rebellious and fractious cabinet; with a Congress sharply divided on the desirable epilogue of the war; with a Supreme Court that had shaped slave power and its strength; with a public opinion that was fundamentally racist and little moved by the

---

[1] Stephen B. Oates, *Builders of the Dream: Abraham Lincoln and Martin Luther King, Jr.*, 1.

fate of the enslaved, if one excepts the abolitionists; and abroad with foreign powers who would have seized the opportunity to weaken the United States for their own advantage.

It is all the more remarkable that Lincoln achieved the feat of rescuing the soul of America without weakening its republican institutions. Even in the few instances in which he resorted to strong powers, he did so as exceptional measures of war, then returned the powers to their appropriate source of expressions.

This book will look both at the Civil War and at the president; at what came before and what followed. Chapter 1 will recapture the nature of the American experiment as can be gleaned from the two iconic figures of Franklin and Washington. It will explore what was achieved and what was left unfinished.

Chapter 2 will look at an Illinois childhood and youth, and the forces that stirred an unusual personality, trying to bring forth very remarkable soul faculties. It will explore how such a youth is emblematic of the American experience, and how everything was being prepared for the coming challenges.

The momentous confrontation between North and South and the place that slavery and its extension took in the national debate and in the soul of America is addressed in Chapter 3. Outright decadence, or personal compromise for political gain, were tearing the last threads of the past asunder.

Chapter 4 will outline the forces that brought Lincoln to the presidency and the forces arrayed against him. The next chapter, the largest, will explore what that presidency did for the nation, what the Civil War meant in the eyes of Lincoln, and what it can mean for us, his successors.

Chapter 6 will assess what Lincoln's work achieved and what ground it laid for the next American national confrontations. The deeper mission and being of Lincoln will be tentatively explored in the conclusions.

Chapter 1

The Forerunners: Washington, Franklin, and the American Revolution

THE REVOLUTIONARY WAR AND THE Constitutional Convention were some of the most thorough processes of education and growth a nation has known in the epoch of the Consciousness Soul. For minds that solely evaluate results with the hindsight of more than two centuries, much could be felt wanting. They could bemoan all the injustices that were not addressed, or everything that was not achieved, as if a social change could achieve everything at once. If we truly look at the change undergone by the national consciousness, something enormous and unique will emerge.

In my previous work *Legends and Stories for a Compassionate America*, the symptomatic approach to history has brought the focus on two truly unique individualities and their collaboration in molding unique historical events and circumstances. We will review briefly some of the outstanding personality traits and historical circumstances before attempting to look at the deeper dimension of the two individuals.

British Imperialism

The relationship of the American colonies to the crown was one of economic domination and extraction of resources. On the surface the American Revolution has been imputed to rebellion against the Stamp Act, the

Townsend Acts, and the Navigation Acts. However, these were merely the last straw of a systematic economic exploitation.

In effect the Council of Trade, later the Board of Trade, had been established in 1660, with the goal of regulating most economic transactions. All American produce could only be exported to Britain, or through Britain, via established monopolies that made very large profits. Imports to the colonies were subject to duties. The balance of trade generated an estimated 30 million pounds in England's favor between 1770 and 1773 alone.[2] Much of English political elites depended on the largesse of the economic monopolies, which they supported.

In order to maintain this economic advantage, the Board of Trade repeatedly prohibited colonial manufacturing activities, criminalized smuggling, and curtailed territorial expansion. Searches without warrant and trials without jury were commonplace.

In such a system of economic injustice, slavery was a natural outgrowth. It entered full force with the cultivation of tobacco, for which the Virginia Company obtained monopoly rights of exportation to England and Ireland. England extended its slave market after prevailing over the Dutch. The slave trade in the southern colonies was regulated by English laws.

Against this background stood two towering figures: Benjamin Franklin and George Washington.

Benjamin Franklin, the First American

The eighteenth century was that of the growing separation between science and faith. Franklin (1706–1790) was an exception, not in the quality of a straggler, but in that of a trailblazer. When he spoke of philosophy, he meant what applied to understanding of external nature as well as human nature, moral and spiritual. And his commitment to knowledge ranged from the philosophical to the practical.

Much of the maturation of Franklin's mind occurred in his twenties. As an alert individual of his time, he could not simply accept faith and disregard science. In fact this meant doubting the truth of the Bible from age fifteen to foregoing church attendance at twenty-four. Two years earlier he had written

---

[2] Douglas Southall Freeman, *Washington: An Abridgment of the 7-Volume Opus*, 154.

his *Articles of Belief and Acts of Religion*, shortly followed by a resolve to form a "United Party for Virtue."

Franklin purported to balance the role of reason, subordinating right action to right thinking, with that of a dispassionate self-analysis. He saw that reason could be led astray by passion, ambition, and pride, and that only a determined effort at self-knowledge could counter this danger. This is what he did in devising to follow thirteen virtues (temperance, order, silence, resolution, frugality, industry, sincerity, justice, moderation, cleanliness, tranquility, chastity, and humility) rigorously in weekly succession; each virtue was thus practiced four times a year. To these he added experiments in abstaining from meat and alcohol, a very unusual interest for an individual of the eighteenth century.

We could say that Franklin strove to be a scientist of inner development rather than relying on faith alone. He had devised a path that no longer rested on dogma, but rather on individual consciousness and effort. It was thus normal that Franklin found his home in the old, though quite diminished, esoteric path of Freemasonry, rather than in a church. He became the Grand Master of Philadelphia's Masonic Lodge in 1834.

Franklin's life came to a turning point when, in the company of radical free thinkers in London, he set out to prove "in a hundred axioms that he knew neither sin, nor liberty, nor personal immortality. God was only permitted to exist as a machine." He felt this had been his personal abyss, and soon after an attack of pleurisy brought him close to death. He gained a concrete experience of the spirit instead, about which he wrote: "I suffered a good deal, gave up the point in my mind, and was rather disappointed when I found myself recovering; regretting in some degree that I must now some time or other have all that disagreeable work to do over again." No doubt this pivotal experience allowed him to write shortly after his own epitaph, in which he said about his own body that "it will (as he believ'd) Appear once More in a New and More Elegant Edition Revised and Corrected by the Author." All in all extraordinary utterances for an eighteenth-century American, or rather a soon-to-be American.

In quick succession Franklin's genius developed in one direction after another. In his youth he formed the Junto, or Leather Apron Club, an association in which participants debated questions of science, philosophy, politics, and business.

In the realm of science Franklin delivered insights in that which would be so important in America's future: electricity. To him we owe the concepts of positive and negative charge. It may be astonishing to realize that Franklin created with ease what only trained mathematicians could: the so-called magic squares, series of seemingly random sequences of number in a grid of 8 rows by 8 columns. The sum of the numbers on each column, row, and even diagonal had to be constant. Not only was this done with ease by Franklin, but he could also replicate the feat in 16 X 16 squares. Moreover, in the technical/ artistic field we owe Franklin the development of the harmonium, perhaps a bit unwieldy as an instrument, but one still used for its unique sonority.

As much as he could have excelled in purely speculative pursuits, Franklin had a gift for anything of a practical and social nature as well. Through the agency of the Junto, Franklin developed the Philadelphia Lending Library and the American Philosophical Society. Around the problem of fire alone he developed a series of innovations, such as the stove that bears his name and the lightning rod. On a social level these were followed by the Union Fire Company, and by the revolutionary idea of the Union Fire Insurance Company, through which he could reach an even larger population.

However, most of all Franklin excelled in the wit of his word and in the promotion of ideas through the printing press, his chosen vocation. It was through his *Poor Richard's Almanac* that Franklin's wisdom found a way into the colonists' hearts. Here was condensed wisdom, along with regular doses of humor to make it easier to remember and assimilate. It was Franklin's declared intention to "leave a strong impression on the memory of young persons."[3]

In his early forties Franklin rose to national and international prominence, working patiently to sow seeds and wait for their time to sprout forth, relinquishing paternity of his ideas in the best of the spirit of Freemasonry.

After traveling to London and earnestly trying to see himself as a man of a larger empire, he gradually realized the obstacles and shackles laid by British imperialism upon its colonies. He became a "reluctant incendiary," protected as he was by a growing reputation, popularity, and the weapon of his humor.

---

[3] Esmond Wright, ed., *Benjamin Franklin: His Life as He Wrote It*, 102.

Benjamin Franklin's 16 X 16 Magic Square

A very interesting 16x16 magic square created by Benjamin Franklin is the one you see below.

208	217	232	249	8	25	40	57	72	89	104	121	136	153	168	185
58	39	26	7	250	231	218	199	186	167	154	135	122	103	90	71
198	219	238	251	6	27	38	59	70	91	102	123	134	155	166	187
60	37	28	5	252	229	220	197	188	165	156	133	124	101	92	69
201	216	233	248	9	24	41	56	73	88	105	120	137	152	169	184
55	42	23	10	247	234	215	202	183	170	151	138	119	106	87	74
203	214	235	246	11	22	43	54	75	86	107	118	139	150	171	182
53	44	21	12	245	236	213	204	181	172	149	140	117	108	85	76
205	212	237	244	13	20	45	52	77	84	109	116	141	148	173	180
51	46	19	14	243	238	211	206	179	174	147	142	115	110	83	78
207	210	239	242	15	18	47	50	79	82	111	114	143	146	175	178
49	48	17	16	241	240	209	208	177	176	145	144	113	112	81	80
196	221	228	253	4	29	36	61	68	93	100	125	132	157	164	189
62	35	30	3	254	227	222	195	190	163	158	131	126	99	94	67
194	223	226	255	2	31	34	63	66	95	98	127	130	159	162	191
64	33	32	1	256	225	224	193	192	161	160	129	128	97	96	65

Although the diagonals of this square do not add up to 2056, there are many other constant properties:

- All the rows and columns sum to the number 2056
- Half rows and half columns sum to 1028.
- The sixteen entries in every 4x4 sub-square sum to 2056.
- the 9 bent diagonals (of 16 cells each) going from top to bottom, 9 from bottom to top, 9 from right to left, 9 from left to right sum to 2056. One example is given for each of the four directions in the square.

See https://www.math.wichita.edu/~richardson/franklin.html for more.

From his pen emerged subtle but scathing criticisms of British imperialism. The first, timid attempt came through his 1751 *Observations Concerning the Increase of Mankind, Peopling of the Countries, etc.* Other, stronger criticism followed, at times under the disguise of a pen-name, such as in *An Edict of the King of Prussia*, and *Rules by Which a Great Empire May Be Reduced to a Small One.*

The latter document, which listed in twenty points the complaints of the colonists against the mother country, has been considered a forerunner of the Declaration of Independence, in whose drafting Franklin played an important role. At this point Franklin had seen in spirit everything that would lead to American independence and had quietly sown the seeds in powerfully measured words.

When the Revolutionary War broke out, Franklin continued his message in France, supporting diplomatically with popular endorsement the campaign of education that Washington was waging on the battlefront. In the schooling of French diplomacy Franklin evolved a new style of international relations focused on economic reciprocity, thus prevailing against other prominent Americans still mired in the habits of delicate political alliances and balances of power.

George Washington

Once the message of independence had been spread, it was George Washington, practically a generation younger than Franklin, who, more than anybody else, carried it further as the commander-in-chief. It was not just the conduct of war that fell into his hands, but also the embodiment of a new role.

If the idea of America was to have a chance, Washington had to be a new kind of general. This he did by molding a new and unified identity among soldiers who had seen themselves as belonging primarily to one of the colonies, and by taking directions and support from a weak and divided Continental Congress. In the process he had to accept inefficient and insufficient support for his military campaigns and the consequent hardships, plus internal divisions. For a man of his stature this meant foregoing the temptation to use his personal charisma or imposing his will, all in service of an idea that had not been tested. At a time in which Napoleon would crown himself emperor, Washington was able to withstand the temptation offered to him to be crowned as king in 1782 by Colonel Lewis Nicola in the name of the army. The effort of education toward the embodiment of new cultural values had to be continuously repeated.

George Washington stood out in contrast to Franklin with an unusually strong physical constitution, inured to prolonged effort, which exposed him to brushes with illness and near confrontations with death. He too joined Freemasonry early on, and it provided him with a code of honor in all his deeds. This spiritual rooting was also echoed in an active life of prayer, and deep spiritual leanings.

Whereas Franklin had to overcome naivete, Washington's test was that of a very strong will and ambition, which he exerted in his life as a Southern planter and as an officer in the colonial army. Not surprisingly Washington's maturation came from the realization of the nature of imperial economics.

As a Southern planter he knew what it meant to be indebted through a captive tobacco market to the British monopolies. And as a member of the Virginia House of Burgesses, twice dissolved during his tenure, he knew how precarious was the colonists' hold on power. In response he joined the colonies' nonimportation agreements as a reaction to the Stamp Act, which imposed a tax on printed materials.

In his lands at Mount Vernon, Washington gradually turned away from tobacco monoculture toward an integrated system of crops and rotations to which he added microenterprises, showing that he knew political independence to be linked to a degree of economic self-sufficiency.

Learning to temper his will, Washington first led the Continental Army to success in the War of Independence, then continued to model the unprecedented role of a national president. Here he guarded the nation against the dangers coming from France in the form of its revolution and from England in the continuing reality of a world economy dominated by English economic and financial channels.

When the 1793 war erupted between France and England, Washington charted a course of strict neutrality that was crucial to the destiny of the new nation. On one hand he had to withstand the allure of the French Revolution upon the minds of the young nation; on the other he made necessary concessions to England in the Jay Treaty of 1794, which were unpopular but allowed the nation to restore peace and disentangle itself from the European dynamics of power, which would have weakened it.

George Washington, Entrepreneur

Washington was a forerunner of what we would call today organic farming and microenterprises.

Organic Farming

Washington's first step was to abandon tobacco, the most common cash crop in Virginia. He stopped because of taxes and duties leveraged on it, and because tobacco monoculture was hurting Mount Vernon's soil. He experimented with as many as sixty different grain crops before choosing wheat as his new mainstay.

Washington recognized the value of compost to enrich the soil. He also experimented with a seven-year crop rotation plan. The rotation, in tandem with the compost practices, greatly improved the long-term productivity of the farms.

Since the farms at Mount Vernon were not adequately prepared for the new grain-based system, Washington set about constructing three major new barn complexes, one to serve the Ferry and French's farms, a second at Dogue Run, and a third at River Farm.

Microenterprises

Mount Vernon ground the grain into flour in a newly minted automated grist mill. It was packaged and branded "G. Washington." It was sold throughout North America, the Caribbean, and Britain. And much of it sailed aboard his own oceangoing sailboats.

The wheat fields supported a profitable whiskey distillery enterprise, whose average 11,000 gallons annual production was one of the largest in America.

Mount Vernon's own textile industry wove the nets for its own fishing enterprise. During the annual spring breeding runs of shad and herring, Washington harvested a two-mile-wide river section on the Potomac for weeks with its own fishing fleet of small boats. In a good year it would catch about 1.5 million. The catch was gutted, salted, and packed into barrels. What could not be used of the fish was recycled as fertilizer for the crops.

As he did with the foreign relations, so did Washington find a middle ground between key individuals in his administration. A foremost example was that of the antagonism between Secretary of State Thomas Jefferson and Secretary of the Treasury Alexander Hamilton. The former was an idealist who succumbed to the appeal of French revolutionaries and a strong supporter of states' rights; the latter a sober and ambitious realist who supported a strong central government and an organization of finances along the British model. The first was able to secure the nation's recognition on the international stage, while the second chartered the nation's financial independence, even though not completely without risks. The president showed that he could mediate between strong personalities in his cabinet without caving in to their agendas.

Unique in his time, Washington was able to live by example his complete alignment of ideas and means, by exerting power during two terms and then relinquishing it. He embodied for all his successors the republican ideals that America wanted to model for the world, not a small departure for a world used to the lifelong power of kings. Through such renunciation the world first came to know what strength could reside in "government of the people, by the people."

The ways in which the two towering individuals collaborated is hidden from immediate scrutiny. It shows us that the elder could not have reached his aims without the younger one. In 1780 Washington could tell from the battlefield that American success hinged on financial support from France, if the colonies wanted to avoid being forced to peace with England. This he wrote to Franklin, and this is what Franklin secured through his diplomatic abilities and popularity among the French people.

It was Franklin who once again stepped in for a momentous decision in proposing Washington as president of the Constitutional Convention. Given Washington's proven integrity and the many links forged with an estimated two thirds of the delegates, be it in politics or in war, his presence and role contributed to bringing out the best in each individual. Franklin's presence, on the other hand, was instrumental in defusing tensions at their incipience, offering alternatives in moments of impasse and appropriate injections of wisdom, levity, and humor. The two iconic figures set a tone for an unprecedented political process.

A Process of National Education

All kinds of distances needed to be bridged at the Constitutional Convention; between small and large states, between individuals and special interests, but most of all between slave and nonslave states.

The civility of the proceedings and the tolerance toward each view expressed were ensured by strict rules of speaking and listening. Considering that the convention gathered for four months under the hot Philadelphia summer sun with hardly any record of emotional outbursts gives us an inkling of the size of the accomplishment.

The fledgling Constitution was then submitted to the will of the people, not just the states, in a continuing process of discussion, education, and improvement. Franklin expressed the ambition of the attempt thus: "To get the bad customs of a country changed, and new ones, though better, introduced, it is necessary first to remove the prejudices of the people, enlighten their ignorance, and convince them that their interests will be promoted by the proposed changes; and this is not the work of one day."

The four months of the convention turned into the ten of the ratification process, months in which the people had ample opportunity to educate themselves, raise questions and objections, and offer ideas for improvement in what was a truly emergent and collective process. It was from the opposition that such an essential addition as the Bill of Rights originated, one that could benefit and satisfy most, if not everybody.

A Closer Look at Franklin and Washington

In 1764 Franklin was quite aptly named the First American.[4] Only later was the term heard in relation to Washington. For the American mind it is quite natural to discern Washington's deeds more readily than those of Franklin. Still, America was first conceived as an idea, and that was Franklin's contribution. And when all is said and done, we can intuit that we stand in front of two "first ones."

Both Washington and Franklin were groomed in the American school of business. For Franklin this had been the enterprise of the printing press

---

[4] Esmond Wright, *Franklin of Philadelphia*, 354.

and the written or spoken word; for Washington farming and fighting. Both had politics in common. The message of the older man of ideas was fully embraced and carried through in action by Washington, the man of the will.

When such larger-than-life individuals present themselves on the stage of history, we can suspect the presence of past initiations. Even though initiation had been rendered practically impossible at the height of materialistic influences and conditions in the eighteenth and nineteenth centuries, we can faintly detect the echoes of initiations in previous incarnations by the tenor of the lives of exceptional individuals, whose path seems to draw them to the right time and the right place in an almost mapped and unavoidable course. In Franklin we see an initiate of the mind and of the word; in Washington one of the will and of the deed. Franklin spoke of the new ideas in two continents; Washington embodied the new ideas through example. The two formed the perfect complement for others like Mason, Madison, Jefferson, and Hamilton to join and offer their best contributions.

What we can say here is naturally of the nature of educated guess. In Franklin we have a unique spirituality that is turned to the world of the soul, to science, and to the external world. In this towering genius Eugen Kolisko recognizes a man able to join the streams of Quakerism, so powerfully impelled by William Penn, and the remaining strength of the Freemason stream.[5]

We can sense the complexion of a Rosicrucian initiate, someone who has worked with matter from a spiritual perspective, someone who can intuit the hidden relationships in nature; witness Franklin's perception of electricity. Moreover, notice his familiarity with the world of numbers, as in resolving the magic squares, and the wisdom present in the simplest of his utterances.

Unfortunately, to my knowledge Steiner has not left us an example of what such a reincarnation could look like, other than the example of Goethe, "whose karma for what is at the moment his latest incarnation was elaborated chiefly in the sphere of the Jupiter wisdom."[6] In Grecian times Goethe had been a sculptor who could perceive imaginatively the etheric forces shaping the human body. Franklin's make-up speaks Jupiter wisdom too.

---

[5] Eugen Kolisko, "Benjamin Franklin."

[6] Rudolf Steiner, *Karmic Relationships*, Volume 6, lecture of June, 1, 1924.

Washington's greatness manifests in a more intimate inner knowing that reveals itself in action. Here fortunately we have an example of known incarnations studied by Steiner, that of Giuseppe Garibaldi, who achieved Italy's liberation almost singlehandedly, without an official military training or a specific mandate from a sovereign of the time.

Garibaldi repeated Washington's step of relinquishing power almost a century later. Like his American counterpart he seemed immune to the lure of power. Steiner attributes such a strength to a previous initiation in what can be called the Mysteries of the West and of Saturn, the Mysteries of Hibernia.

The Mysteries of Hibernia led the candidates through long trials to a supersensible knowledge of the far past and far future of Earth evolution through the Saturn beings. "Saturn Beings may therefore be characterized by saying that they gaze back upon memory, if I may express it, of all the beings of the whole planetary system. Everything is inscribed in this faculty of cosmic remembrance, cosmic memory of the Saturn Beings."[7] Garibaldi was one of the individuals, together with Victor Hugo, whom Steiner closely associated with the activity of the Saturn beings and the Saturn sphere in the journey after death.

Garibaldi was a man of action who carried the inspiration from the Mysteries of Hibernia in an earlier incarnation. He acted from a determination that arose solely from within, and expressed itself with primeval urgency and inner certainty, while to the outside world, his words seemed vague, strange, incomprehensible. Steiner says of him: "Garibaldi is eminently fit to stand with both feet planted firmly on the earth—witness his enormous political achievements—and still seems to hover somehow above the earth, living strongly in his own imaginative world."[8]

After liberating the whole of Italy in a spectacular manner, Garibaldi left the stage of history to retire in the secluded island of Caprera, off the coast of Sardinia. Not only did he turn his back to power in an astounding manner; he also relinquished it in the hand of people who would not necessarily share his views: Giuseppe Mazzini; Camillo Benso, Count of Cavour; and most of all the king Victor Emmanuel of Savoy. Victor Emmanuel, who benefited

---

[7] Rudolf Steiner, *Karmic Relationships*, volume 7, lecture 4 of June 10, 1924.

[8] See Rudolf Steiner, *Karmic Relationships*, volume 7, lecture 5 of June 11, 1924, and *Karmic Relationships*, volume 1, lecture of March 23, 1924.

most from this "gift," hardly had republican leanings. The three individuals had been Garibaldi's pupils in a previous incarnation in the Mysteries of Hibernia, and the Italian liberator acted out of an esoteric inner duty toward them.

We can detect in Washington many of the traits of Garibaldi: an impressive, sheer physical strength and presence; the disregard for danger; a strong sense of mission; together with an inner knowing of what to do in sight of the future that is calling America to be. It takes an initiatic past in order to withstand the untold pressures of a war conducted on so many fronts—from the confrontation with the real enemy to the failures, shortcomings, and betrayals of allies and friends—not to mention the ability to exert power with restraint and in the end relinquish it.

What Was Left Unfinished

It is a true wonder that America was formed in spite of the deeply divisive issue of slavery. Or rather we could say, the greatness of America lay in not seeking perfection, in knowing that only so much could be achieved at a given time; the possible best had to be promoted at the expense of the absolute desirable good.

Where the pursuit of absolute ideals on the social arena has held sway, the outcomes have generally led to brutal bloodshed and repression. The French Revolution, setting the bar for higher and higher ideals, could only lead to succeeding inner coups, to the enamored pursuit of ideal perfection that did not realize the mounting costs of demonizing larger segments of the population through summary executions. When all was lost, a dictator took advantage of the situation and crowned himself emperor.

Much the same could be said of the Russian Revolution in its pursuit of the ideal of the new man and the classless society. The American Revolution in contrast stood for an ideal of radical moderation and constructive compromise. And a compromise, which could and should lead to a later confrontation, was the one reached on slavery. Another one was that of the banking system. What unites both of these is the economic field in which Ahriman imposes his reality.

From an esoteric perspective we must realize that a Luciferic search for perfection leads only to a rude awakening in deprivation of freedom.

Constructive social projects are dated and time-bound. They are what is good enough or the best possible for the times. In the age of the Consciousness Soul we constantly sow seeds in the fields of Ahriman, see what thrives and survives, then watch for the time to sow new seeds. No perfection can be reached once and forever; constant vigilance seems to be the only way to improve a social system.

The Issue of Slavery

In America the Constitutional Convention had achieved remarkable results AND it had sown the seed of a big question that needed to be addressed: What will we do with slavery?

Jefferson's original draft to the Declaration of Independence included a passage condemning King George's support for slavery. This stated:

> He has waged cruel war against human nature itself, violating its most sacred rights of life & liberty in the persons of a distant people who never offended him, captivating & carrying them into slavery in another hemisphere or to incur miserable death in their transportation thither. This piratical warfare, the opprobrium of infidel powers, is the warfare of the Christian King of Great Britain. Determined to keep open a market where Men should be bought & sold, he has prostituted his negative for suppressing every legislative attempt to prohibit or restrain this execrable commerce. And that this assemblage of horrors might want no fact of distinguished die, he is now exciting those very people to rise in arms among us, and to purchase that liberty of which he has deprived them, by murdering the people on whom he also obtruded them: thus paying off former crimes committed against the Liberties of one people, with crimes which he urges them to commit against the lives of another.[9]

---

[9] BlackPast, "(1776) The Deleted Passage of the Declaration of Independence," https://www.blackpast.org/african-american-history/declaration-independence-and-debate-over-slavery/

After intense debate, the passage was removed. Jefferson blamed the removal of the passage not just on the delegates representing the obvious interests of slaveholders but also on Northern slave traders.[10]

Most of the Founders had done everything possible to push slavery toward restriction and eventual extinction. But, on the other hand, the compromise of the Constitution had established the enslaved person not only as an object of trade but also as three fifths of a person to serve the interests of the slaveholders. Sooner or later a new confrontation was bound to happen, and this inevitably led to the Civil War.

Washington and Franklin could not help but see the storms to come. In his 1751 *Observations Concerning the Increase of Mankind, Peopling of the Countries, etc. . . .* Franklin clearly showed his views on slavery: "The labor of slaves can never be so cheap here as the labor of working men in Britain." Franklin was pointing to slavery's real and hidden economic and social costs. And from his larger view of things, he no doubt could imagine the storms to come on such an obvious issue.

Something similar happened to Washington, and here more documentation is available on a variety of places. Washington first witnessed the valor of free Black men fighting in the Continental Army, and he championed their desegregation in the 1st Rhode Island Regiment. He was also impressed by the presence and poetry of freed enslaved person Phyllis Wheatley, who dedicated a poem to him.

More to the point it is Washington who first understood that slavery was not an issue that could be resolved on the political front alone, but at the economic level of a global economy that still linked the United States to England and the reality of economic imperialism. For that reason it is important to consider that after the war the former Middle Colonies took on a major role in the slave trade. Thus slavery was in a truer sense a national problem, not a sectional one alone, caused by a deeply interconnected world economy.

True to himself, Washington did not write about how to address slavery; he just showed what to do by example. In his Mount Vernon estates he

[10] Thomas Jefferson, *The Writings of Thomas Jefferson: Being His Autobiography, Correspondence, Reports, Messages, Addresses, and Other Writings, Official and Private.* See https://www.blackpast. org/african-american-history/declaration-independence-and-debate-over-slavery/

developed a very diversified agricultural economy with microindustries adding value to the produce. He modeled a farming example sustainability and self-reliance. This is what allowed him to achieve what Jefferson wanted to do but couldn't: freeing all his slaves. Washington had deeply understood, no doubt through bitter personal experience, how slavery was the result of a whole economic system deeply degrading for environment and human being alike.

The Issue of Banking

According to the Constitution, it is only Congress that can mint money, not the States: "Congress shall have the power to borrow money . . . to coin money, . . . No state shall . . . coin money, emit bills of credit; [or] make anything but gold and silver coin a tender in payment of debts" (Article 1, Section 8 and 10).

The prohibition of bills of credit refers to the printing of fractional or fiat money not backed by metal. The Constitution does not clearly forbid the federal government from doing so. However, that aim was clear at the time of the writing of the Constitution and in the years that followed.

Let's look back at the matter of issuance of money during the Revolutionary War and in the early days of the Republic. At the beginning of the war in 1775, the total available money in circulation was 12 million continental dollars. By the end of the year, the federated colonies' money supply stood at 18 million dollars; this rose to 64 million in 1778 and 125 million in 1779, or a 2000% increase above the 1775 level. In 1775 the continental was valued at one dollar in gold; in 1779 it was worth less than a penny.[11]

The Bank of North America

This bank had been chartered by Congress in 1781, and it was financed by Robert Morris and others who wanted a strong central government and a model similar to the British. In fact Morris's bank resembled very closely the Bank of England. Though there were limitations placed on the bank, it was awarded a monopoly. The initial subscription required $400,000 in private funds. Morris deposited the gold loaned to the U. S. from France, over 60%

---

[11] G. Edward Griffin, *The Creature from Jekyll Island: A Second Look at the Federal Reserve*, 312.

of the initial subscription. The bank's charter from the state of Pennsylvania was not renewed at the end of the war.

The term *dollar* derives from the Bavarian thaler, though Congress adopted it via the Spanish dollar in June 1785, and defined its weight accurately soon after. Capital punishment was enforced for those who debased the dollar, and citizens could take their own gold or silver to mint. This was called "free coinage," and it lasted until the Gold Reserve Act of 1934.

The First Bank of the United States

The proposal for the successor to the Bank of North America was submitted by Alexander Hamilton, who was a former aide to Morris. The Bank of the United States was given a 20-year charter in 1791. It was almost an exact replica of the Bank of North America. It became the depository of all federal funds and received monopoly power in the printing of notes.

As was common in this type of enterprise, it only collected a modest $675,000 of the initially planned capital of $10 million.[12] Nathan Rothschild had already become the official banker for the U. S. government and naturally supported the bank. In the first five years inflation reached 72%.[13] Gradually political opinion turned against the bank, particularly through the Jeffersonians, though it was also opposed by the "wildcat banks" that wanted to operate beyond any constraints. In 1811, the charter of renewal was defeated by one vote, leaving state-chartered corporations their much-wanted complete financial freedom.

The Second Bank of the United States

In 1816 another 20-year charter was granted to the Second Bank. Here too there was significant presence of foreign investment; a third of the whole came through Great Britain. The Second Bank left private banks able to play the fractional reserve mechanism of lending against their present outstanding loans considered as deposits. The number of banks rose by 46%

---

[12] G. Edward Griffin, *The Creature from Jekyll Island: A Second Look at the Federal Reserve*, 330.

[13] G. Edward Griffin, *The Creature from Jekyll Island: A Second Look at the Federal Reserve*, 335.

by 1819 and the money supply by $27.4 million, corresponding to more than a 40% inflation.[14]

The bank was headed by Nicholas Biddle, a brilliantly precocious mind. He had graduated from the University of Pennsylvania at age thirteen and knew all about the science of money.

By 1818 the bank realized the danger of inflation and decided to curtail credit by calling back old loans and being more conservative on new loans. The very drastic policy of credit contraction caused defaults, bankruptcies, and liquidation of precarious investments. The result was a severe depression.

A fraction of the newly formed Democratic Party in the late 1820s abandoned conservative fiscal policy, led by Van Buren and Jackson; its goal was the abolition of the bank. Andrew Jackson placed this issue at the center of his campaign. He was elected in 1828 with 55% of the popular vote and 68% of the electoral vote.

After the election Biddle antagonized Jackson through contractionary financial policies, hoping to place the blame of the results on Jackson. Biddle, boldly sure of himself, did not refrain from making this challenge public. At the time of renewal of the charter, Jackson won a strong victory in his refusal of the bank. The bank was restructured as the Bank of Pennsylvania, which closed within five years; Biddle was accused of fraud, and he died before the end of the proceedings against him. However, the end of the bank did not usher in a time of sound fiscal policies.

The Michaelic Impulse in America

Alexis de Tocqueville was deeply impressed during his time in the new nation by the social impulse and opportunities that were present in America. Here was a new continent with access to land and resources, freedom of expression in the religious field, and spontaneous cultural associative impulses. Add to this the natural tendency to leave behind the cultural baggage of oppression and wanting to identify to the new possibilities rather

---

[14] G. Edward Griffin, *The Creature from Jekyll Island: A Second Look at the Federal Reserve*, 343.

than the old constraints. This gave the new Americans the concrete feelings of equality regardless of national origin.

Countess Keyserlingk, who was close to Steiner in his later years, shares her perceptions of the spiritual forces at play in America in a short article.[15] Her impressions, though brief, are worth summarizing here. The countess saw the Michaelic impulse that originally tried to found the premises for threefolding in the calls of freedom, equality, and brotherhood of the French Revolution, move to America once the impulse was distorted from its original on French soil: "When the spiritual powers at the end of the eighteenth century saw that this could not be the case, a proportion of the forces that had been intended to work in Europe for threefolding was transferred to America for safekeeping."

Keyserlingk recognizes that the conditions of the new culture were favorable to the Michaelic cosmopolitan impulse. There was freedom in the cultural life and freedom in the expression of the individuality. There was a healthy balance between self-reliance and mutual interdependence. To this was added the impulse to recognize each other as Americans, rather than English, Scots, Germans, French, Dutch, etc.

The above conditions, the countess argues, prevailed between 1791 and 1845, the year that ushered in much of what interests us in this study. She continues, "Thereafter, something like a council of anti-Christian powers must have happened; the earthly effects of this can be seen especially in the years 1843–1850. These were the years that led to the annexation of Texas as a slave territory, the war with Mexico, and the rise of the doctrine of popular sovereignty leading to the Compromise of 1850.

The dangers to come were also perceived, or rather "seen" by George Washington.

Washington's Vision for the Future of the United States

Before moving from the American Revolution to the times of the Civil War, we will cast a glance at a surprising experience and revelation vouchsafed to Washington in the interest of America's future.

In the winter of 1778 at Valley Forge, the fates of Washington and the Continental Army reached their lowest point. Washington, deeply

---

[15] Countess Johanna von Keyserlingk, "Countess Keyserlingk on Spiritual Streams in the USA."

concerned and discouraged, had turned to the life of prayer to try to find hope and meaning. It was here that Washington experienced a vision that offered him a deeply meaningful turning point. He conveyed it to his aide Anthony Sherman, who later contributed to publishing it.[16]

The following are Washington's words as recorded by Sherman: "This afternoon, as I was sitting at this table engaged in preparing a dispatch, something seemed to disturb me. Looking up [in front of the fire] I beheld standing opposite a singularly beautiful female." And further: "My thought itself became paralyzed! A new influence, mysterious, potent, irresistible, took possession of me! All I could do was gaze steadily, vacantly at my unknown visitant."

Washington inquired about the presence's identity four times, but to no avail. Then he saw it assume a new form: "Gradually the surrounding atmosphere seemed filled with sensations, and grew luminous. Everything about me seemed to rarefy; the mysterious visitor herself becoming more airy and yet more distinct to my sight than ever."

Washington's consciousness was noticeably altered, as we hear in his own words: "I next began to feel as one dying, or rather to experience the sensation which I sometimes imagined accompanies dissolution [death]. I did not think, I did not reason. I did not move. All that was impossible. I was conscious only of gazing fixedly at my companion."

With the words "Son of the Republic, look and learn!" the being then took Washington to a landscape in which he saw spread out in front of him the continents of the earth. The angelic figure dipping her hands in water sprinkled some of it over America and some over Europe. From the waters a cloud arose from each landmass. The two first converged over the ocean, then moved west to envelop America. After this process was repeated three times, and the cloud dissipated, Washington saw the landscape grow with villages, towns, and cities.

Washington then beheld prophetic images of times to come:

> And with this the dark, shadowy figure turned its face southward, and from Africa I saw an ill-omened specter approaching our land. It flitted slowly over every city and

---

[16] *National Tribune* (volume 4, number 12), quoted in Susan B. Martinez, *The Psychic Life of Abraham Lincoln*, 87–89.

every town of the latter. The inhabitants presently set themselves in battle against each other. As I continued looking at the bright angel, on whose brow rested a crown of light on which was traced the word "Union," I saw the angel place an American flag between the divided nation, and say, "Remember, ye are brethren." Instantly, the inhabitants, casting from them their weapons, became friends once more, and united around the National Standard.

More followed, to which we will return at the end of our explorations.

In reviewing the whole, Washington came to the conclusion: "... [I] felt I had seen a vision wherein had been shown to me the birth, progress, and destiny of the United States."

Lincoln and Washington

Lincoln ascended to the presidency exactly seventy-two years after Washington did. Even before becoming a lawyer he wrote a prophetic essay on "the necessity of preserving the Constitution and perpetuating the Union."[17] Here we can recognize his intuition of things to come. Elsewhere, Lincoln clearly indicated the continuity of his intent with that of the Founding Fathers, Washington most of all. And this was inextricably bound with a recognition of the hand of providence in historical affairs.

Both themes appear interlinked in his "Farewell Address" upon leaving Springfield: "I now leave, not knowing when, or whether ever, I may return, with a task before me greater than that which rested upon Washington. Without the assistance of that Divine Being who ever attended him, I cannot succeed."

In Trenton, remembering Washington, Lincoln argued that the Revolutionary Fathers had fought for something larger than national independence; rather "something that held promise to all the people of the world for all time to come."[18]

What Lincoln intuited about himself was captured by those who have

---

[17] Albert A. Woldman, *Lawyer Lincoln*, 11.
[18] William J. Wolf, *The Almost Chosen People: A Study of the Religion of Abraham Lincoln*, 117.

a more intuitive consciousness, the poets. R. W. Emerson, who took time in recognizing Lincoln's historical stature, concluded, "Only Washington can compare with him."

This book will be an exploration of the threads that unite the beginnings of the nation with the momentous turning point of Lincoln's presidency and the Civil War.

Chapter 2

An Illinois Youth

THAT LINCOLN'S PERSONALITY PRESENTED MANY unusual aspects and unique contrasts/polarities is something that we will see in more than one way and gather in the next chapters. The first striking aspect was his physical appearance. This was the object of self-deprecating humor that Lincoln practiced so well. One of his classical jokes in this regard was that of a man having made a promise of giving a gift to someone uglier than himself, who had approached him to deliver on his pledge.

In the box in the next page is a description of Lincoln's appearance that would have tickled the man's sense of humor. Here we already see a far-from-common physical constitution and external appearance.

Beyond Lincoln's striking appearance, something unusual expresses itself already in the body. Here was a man of great muscular strength, one who could lift a thousand pounds with no apparent effort, wield an ax with ease like any lumberjack. Curiously, he disliked socks even in winter, tight boots, and tight collars. He would remove his shoes even during meetings.

Consider that he never took a holiday in his four years in office.[19] In his youthful years as a circuit judge he thrived where others struggled and suffered. His work demanded of him to accommodate continuous movement on horseback on rough roads; wading or swimming at river crossings; lack of comfortable lodging, sleep, and food; and the forced company of all sorts of people. None of this affected his jovial spirit. By all standards here was

---

[19] Lincoln's death agony took nine hours for a wound that most would not have survived two hours (David Herbert Donald, *Lincoln*, 598).

a man who was as strong in his will and body as he will see him clear in his thinking and in the pursuits of the mind.

Family Background

Recent research shows that the Lincolns came from Virginia, but earlier generations had lived in Pennsylvania and joined the Society of Friends. The original Samuel Lincoln had emigrated from Norfolk, England, and settled in Hingham, Massachusetts. The grandfather Abraham sold his farm in Virginia and moved to Kentucky, before being killed by Indians. The brother Mordecai saved Thomas, Abraham's father, from an Indian who was about to kill him.

The father Thomas, youngest of the family, did not inherit from the father and had to struggle to save money to buy land. He had little education but was respected for his honesty. Though Nancy Hanks Lincoln was reputed "brilliant" and "intellectual," she probably could read but did not write. Lincoln rarely mentioned her other than to call her his "angel mother."

Lincoln spent the first seven years of his life in Hardin County, Kentucky, where the father was part of the Separate Baptist Church, which opposed slavery. Hardin County counted 1,007 enslaved people and only 1,627 males over the age of 16 in 1811 census.[20]

In 1816, at age seven, Lincoln moved from Kentucky to Indiana, across the Ohio River. The Indiana territory was in the process of being admitted to the Union as a state. One early memory of the young Abraham was that of shooting at a turkey. He later remembered that he had never killed anything larger than that. At about this time he survived the kick of a mare that landed on his forehead and left him unconscious. He was given for dead at first, and was unable to speak for a few hours after. These details give us an idea of the rough environment of the frontier to which Lincoln grew accustomed.

Nancy Hanks died of "milk sickness" in October 1816. The father returned to Kentucky to find a wife, and married Sarah Bush Johnston, a widow with three children. The stepmother treated all children equally and became very fond of Abraham. The child experienced the years with her as joyous. He learned the rudiments of reading and writing, but according to at least one

---

[20] David Herbert Donald, *Lincoln*, 25.

of his cousins, John Hanks, at that time, he was "somewhat dull" though methodic and disciplined in his learning. The stepmother understood how important learning was for Lincoln and how slow and devoted he was with it.

Lincoln was in fact interested in any of the few books he could lay his hands on, on the frontier. In fact the word in all its aspects fascinated him. From early on one could detect his faculty for telling stories or jokes, writing poems, and public speaking. Among his favorites was the rendition of sermons parodying the preachers who offered them. He also naturally tended to take on the role of leader.

A First Impression of Lincoln

"To say he is ugly is nothing; to add that his figure is grotesque is to convey no adequate description. Fancy a very tall man with long bony arms and legs which somehow seem to always be in the way; with great rugged furrowed hands which grasp you like a vice when shaking yours; a long scraggly neck and a chest too narrow for the great arms at his side.

"Add to this figure a head, coconut shaped, that is somewhat too small for his stature and covered with rough, uncombed hair standing out in every direction; a face furrowed, wrinkled and indented as though it had been scarred by vitriol; a high narrow forehead sunk beneath bushy eyebrows with too bright, somewhat dreamy eyes, that seem to gaze at you without looking at you; a few irregular blotches of black bristly hairs where beard and whiskers ought to grow; a stern close-set, thin-lipped mouth with two rows of large white teeth and a nose and ears which have been mistakenly taken from a head twice the size.

"Clothe him in a long, tight, badly-fitting black suit that is creased, soiled and puckered at every salient point. Then add large ill-fitting boots, gloves too long for his long bony fingers and a tall hat covered with dusty puffy crepe. And when you are finished critiquing this woe-struck image, add an ironic air of both physical and moral strength with a dignity that incongruously pairs with grotesqueness. That is the impression left upon you by Abraham Lincoln."

Joseph E. Stevens in *The Rebirth of a Nation*.

As his father grew old and his health declined, he became more and more dependent on Abraham, who would be hired to work for other neighboring farmers in order to bring back his earnings to the family.

At age nineteen Lincoln joined James Gentry on a river boat trip to New Orleans to sell a cargo of meat, corn, and flour. Arriving in New Orleans, Lincoln saw a great number of enslaved people. The issue of slavery marked in fact an early divider in Lincoln's life; he was born in slave state, before moving to Indiana and Illinois, both free states.

Self-Education

Lincoln had little access to more than the rudiments of reading and writing and the basic education of frontier life. But once he learned to read and write, encouraged by the stepmother Sarah, he first approached the Bible, then *Lessons in Elocution* by William Scott, where he was probably also introduced to Shakespeare. Soon after he enjoyed both Franklin's autobiography and the then classic Parson Mason Weems's *Life of George Washington*.

Something was already showing of the inextricably linked desire for lifelong learning and love of the word. As a child he had already formed the habit of writing words and sentences on whatever medium he could find available, even in sand and snow. Otherwise he would read everything he could, and rewrite passages that would catch his attention, then repeat them. Such was his obsession for grasping the full meaning of a word that he would get irritated when spoken to in a way he could not understand. The prevailing need for accurate understanding of words also transferred to the realm of ideas. Later on as a circuit lawyer he developed the unique habit of reading while barefoot and leaning against a tree, or lying on his back and resting his feet on the tree. He would carry a book while walking and turn to it if not otherwise engaged.

The word provided the youth not just meaning but also the pleasure of its sound. Lincoln's rhetorical art, later so eloquently expressed in writing, was mostly learned from speaking. Even when he read he liked to do it aloud to reinforce what he saw with what he heard; he felt it deepened his learning. Naturally this led him to using all opportunities for delivering skits, impersonations, or public speeches. Together with an uncommon memory for details, he could mimic and repeat gestures, intonations, and accents. In fact such was Lincoln's memory that he could even remember the names, residences, and family connections of people called to jury duty when he was a lawyer.

With all of the above in mind, it is not surprising to find in Lincoln's youth early literary ambitions. His first attempts were at comic verses and satire, such as the *Chronicles of Reuben*, a parody of the biblical account that referred to a pretentious wedding reception. At the other end, and in a typical fashion for the person, he also wrote a poem about suicide, published anonymously in 1838 in the *Sangamo Journal*. His most ambitious effort formed the three "Indiana poems" that were inspired by his residence in the state. Douglas L. Wilson contrasts the "somewhat mechanical versification" with the "rather interesting and complex ideas" and "strong sense of cadence and sophisticated ear for rhythmic patterns," all in all quite surprising for a youth with little exposure to formal education.[21]

Love for poetry was to be a constant throughout his life, from Shakespeare to Robert Burns, and many in between, such as Oliver Wendell Holmes, William Knox, and Longfellow. He memorized many of their poems or passages. Among his favorites were Longfellow's *Hiawatha*, Emerson's *Representative Men*, and Plutarch's *Lives*.

Like Franklin before him, Lincoln immersed himself in the reading and understanding of the Bible on one hand, and in the freethinkers on the other, studying Thomas Paine's *Age of Reason* and Constantin de Volney's *Ruins of Empires*. In addition he read eclectically from Kant to Renan, Fichte, Buckle, and Froude. When he was accused of being a "heretic," he issued a formal denial, where, among other things, he claimed, "That I am not a member of any Christian church is true; but I have never denied the truth of Scriptures."[22]

Learning took on other forms: when confronted with some professional ambition, he would naturally tackle it through self-learning. Wanting to become county surveyor, he started teaching himself trigonometry. After being hired he took on progressively harder assignments. When given the opportunity to become a lawyer, he took learning in his own hand and never ceased, even when president.

---

[21] Douglas L. Wilson, *Lincoln's Sword: The Presidency and the Power of Words*, 24.

[22] David Herbert Donald, *Lincoln*, 51.

In his love for the word, Lincoln dedicated himself to improving his knowledge of grammar. But his appetite for learning went also toward astronomy, mathematics, and geometry, and not just in a superficial way! The love for geometry led him to reading the six books of Euclid and becoming able to demonstrate the theorems.

Frontier Man Seeking a Vocation

Much has been said of Lincoln as the example of the self-made man, and of his time as a "rail-splitter." As his father was getting old, Lincoln hired himself out for a great variety of jobs to supply to the family needs. His biographer, David Herbert Donald, lists among his employments those of carpenter, riverboat man, store clerk, merchant, postmaster, blacksmith, surveyor, and clerk at elections, to which we could add officer in the militia, before finding his vocation in the twin professions of lawyer and politician. For this reason he used to call himself a "piece of floating driftwood." Here was a man preeminently fit to the life of the frontier. His skills for observation, prodigious memory, and keen thinking were already leaving their mark. Lincoln's practical mind even produced a patented invention.

In 1830 Lincoln helped his parents move from Spencer County, Indiana, to Macon County, Illinois. Apparently at this time he made his first political speech, addressing a campaign meeting in Decatur. Already at that time, it was clear that he was perfectly comfortable on stage. In parallel he also started participating in the New Salem debating club and showed a keen eagerness for learning.

Part of what allowed Lincoln to move from one thing to another before finding his way was his gregariousness. This in fact played a role in his first study of the law, as we will see shortly. When Lincoln arrived in New Salem, Illinois, the town that had only been founded two years before, serving as a commercial crossroads supplying the rural areas. Lincoln soon found his place with his stories and his humor. He also displayed courage in winning over the rough sort of the frontier.

Lincoln the Inventor and Patent 6,469

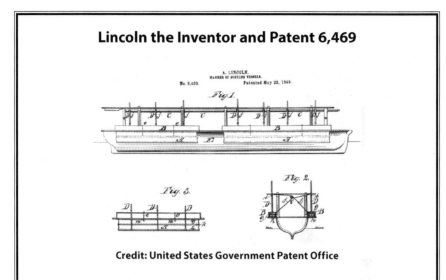

Credit: United States Government Patent Office

The registered patent No. 6,469 reads,

"Be it known that I, Abraham Lincoln, of Springfield, in the county of Sangamon, in the state of Illinois, have invented a new and improved manner of combining adjustable buoyant air chambers with a steam boat or other vessel for the purpose of enabling their draught of water to be readily lessened to enable them to pass over bars, or through shallow water, without discharging their cargoes."

The invention originated from the episode in which Lincoln's flatboat got grounded over the Rutledge milldam, south of New Salem while he was sailing down the Sangamon River in April 1831. The boat was taking water from the rear while the front hung over the dam. Lincoln borrowed an auger and drilled a hole in the back of the boat. At the same time he proceeded to roll some of the barrels toward the prow, and to unroll the hogs on a neighboring boat. The whole ordeal took half a day and one night.

From this experience it was natural that Lincoln would develop interest in developing an invention for boats to float when passing over shallow waters, or free themselves once stranded. His idea was to simply place inflatable chambers just below the boat's water line, and inflate them through a system of shafts, ropes, and pulleys. He devoted quite some energy to the project and sent a model for a patent to Washington.

From Jason, Emerson, *Lincoln the Inventor.*

Together with humor, Lincoln had a keen clarity of mind, and he started helping his neighbors with legal advice and the drafting of simple legal documents. In 1832 James Rutledge suggested that he run for state legislature, and Lincoln took him up on it. At this point in the life of Illinois, the differences between Democrats and Whigs had not acquired great importance yet. Lincoln ran an announcement in the local *Sangamon Journal*, proposing improvements on the navigability of the Sangamon River. In his campaign he used the word "humble" to refer to himself, as he would do on another thirty-five occasions at least before 1860.[23] Although he was only eighth of thirteen candidates, the fact that in New Salem he received 277 out of 300 votes indicates the range of his social skills and network.

Lincoln's initial political ambition was affected by the failure of Denton Offutt's business venture, which he had joined, selling corn seed, cottonseed, and hogs. Left unemployed, Lincoln was lucky to be enrolled in the militia to fight against Black Hawk and his four hundred fifty Sauk and Fox warriors who wanted to reclaim their ancestral homeland. His men soon elected him officer. A popular leader, he also displayed courage in standing his ground against those among his men who wanted to kill a Native American who bore a "certificate of good character" from American authorities. During this time his reputation grew, and he entered in contact with rising political leaders. An important karmic connection was formed at this stage with John Stuart Todd, a Springfield lawyer.

After the militia episode Lincoln entered a partnership with William F. Berry. Together they owned one of the three stores in New Salem, supplying coffee, tea, sugar, salt, and whiskey, together with such things such as hats, textiles, and shoes. When the commercial venture failed, Lincoln was appointed village postmaster and held some other odd jobs before becoming county surveyor.

Lincoln the Politician

In 1834 Lincoln presented himself again for the state legislature. Although he enthusiastically supported Henry Clay's American System—including a national tariff to protect American industry, a national bank, and federal

---

[23] David Herbert Donald, *Lincoln*, 44.

subsidies for roads, canals, and other "internal improvements"—he did not campaign openly on this platform. In fact this was a political calculation because most of his electorate were Democrat farmers who favored Andrew Jackson.

Lincoln came in second among thirteen candidates and was elected to one of the four vacant seats. He prepared for his new job by studying the law. He had to travel to Vandalia, the then capital of the state. He soon understood enough to be able to draft bills and assist his colleagues in doing so. Though he was now generating a better income, his joint venture with Berry had gone bankrupt and Lincoln was left with half the debts. When Berry died soon after, Lincoln agreed to pay the whole amount owed.

In a major initiative of the legislature, Lincoln supported the building of a canal connecting the Illinois to the Chicago River, creating access to Lake Michigan and the Mississippi. The measure was narrowly approved. The new legislator then became an open supporter of internal improvements and the American System proposed by Henry Clay. This view advocated that the federal government implement protective tariffs and promote internal improvements and a national bank to develop the nation's economy.

In 1836 Lincoln was reelected to the Illinois General Assembly and also received his license to practice law. Though Lincoln was the next to youngest, he was chosen as the Whigs' floor leader. Stephen Douglas had just been elected from Morgan County (Jacksonville) and assumed local leadership of the Democratic Party at age twenty-three! He was a supporter and promoter of a train line connecting the north to the south of the state as well as of the Illinois and Michigan canals. At that time there was also a measure to condemn and ban abolitionist societies—Illinois's population was mostly of Southern origin—and Lincoln voted against it.

Lincoln was starting to bring together his oratorical, writing, and social skills. He wrote "The Perpetuation of Our Political Institutions" in the *Sangamo Journal* in which he copied the conventional flowery prose of his time. Two years later in a political speech on the Federal Sub-Treasury he was already abandoning this style to get into his own. He proved that he could render clear and alive complex issues that lacked immediate appeal. He was able to expose a complex fraud in a brief, succinct way. One could see that putting things into writing was for him a way to come to clarity and help others do the same.

Another facet of Lincoln's unique outlook already comes to the fore in the address given to Springfield's Washington Temperance Society. It outlines the man's views about how to convince and motivate people to change. As in many other places throughout his presidency Lincoln managed to find a constructive medium between opposites: although he did not drink, he did not support the Prohibitionist movement. He was in favor of the "persuasion, kind, unassuming persuasion" professed by the Washingtonian Society. With great insight he pointed out to the role of the reformed alcoholic and his mission to the fellow sufferers. He added that it was important to approach the alcoholic as a true friend first of all; accusation, as it was currently practiced, was not only untactful but also unjust. He brought his reasoning to a pitch thus: "If they [Christians] believe, as they profess, that Omnipotence condescended to take on himself the form of sinful man, and as such, to die an ignominious death for their sakes, surely they would not refuse submission to the infinitely lesser condescension, for the temporal, and perhaps eternal salvation, of a large, erring, and unfortunate class of their own fellow creatures."

Hearing Lincoln speak was quite an experience. His high-pitched voice turned even more shrill when he became excited. It could be heard at the farthest reaches of a large crowd gathered outdoors. And he often accompanied it with considerable body language. He had a great sense of timing and could feel the mood of a jury or crowd. Add to this a great memory for facts, figures, anecdotes, and humorous stories.

In his law practice Lincoln was known for a quick wit, but also for a slow, deliberate thinking. He would plead for time in presenting his cases to make sure he could gather all evidence and present his position convincingly.

On a more informal basis, Lincoln had the gift of making everyone felt welcome and at ease. His wit and humor won people over. He made the conversation agreeable with stories and anecdotes and often had the last word. He could pull the right story for the right moment at will, and knew that common folk were more easily influenced through these than through logical arguments.

Lincoln the Orator

Concerning Lincoln's Cooper Institute Address of February 27, 1860, to a crowd of some 1,500 people, George Haven Putnam, reporting for the *New York Herald*, wrote:

"When Lincoln rose to speak, I was greatly disappointed. He was tall, tall, oh so tall, and so angular and awkward that I had for an instant a feeling of pity for so ungainly a man. He began in a low tone of voice, as if he were used to speaking out-of-doors, and was afraid of speaking too loud.

He said, 'Mr. Cheerman,' instead of 'Mr. Chairman,' and employed many other words with an old-fashioned pronunciation. I said to myself, "Old fellow, you won't do; it is all very well for the Wild West, but this will never go down in New York." But pretty soon he began to get into the subject; he straightened up, made regular and graceful gestures; his face lighted as with an inward fire; the whole man was transfigured. I forgot the clothing, his personal appearance, and his individual peculiarities. Presently, forgetting myself, I was on my feet with the rest, yelling like a wild Indian, cheering the wonderful man. In the close parts of his argument, you could hear the gentle sizzling of the gas burners [used for lighting].

When he reached a climax, the thunders of applause were terrific. It was a great speech. It was a great speech. When I came out of the hall, my face glowing with excitement and my frame all a-quiver, a friend, with his eyes aglow, asked me what I thought of Abe Lincoln. I said: 'He's the greatest man since St. Paul.'"

Having entered the field of law through politics, Lincoln was officially licensed in 1836. He moved to Springfield, the new capital of the state.

Lincoln the Lawyer

Lincoln's love for the law took its blessing from the reading of the Blackstone's Commentaries (see box next page). To present readers, the commentaries may be just any book of law. For men of the nineteenth century, a library was considered complete if next to the Bible and Shakespeare it counted Blackstone's Commentaries, to encompass the best of religion, philosophy, and law.[24]

---

[24] Albert A. Woldman, *Lawyer Lincoln*, 17.

At age twenty-eight Lincoln was offered a partnership as a lawyer with Major John Todd Stuart, cousin of his future wife Mary Todd. He remained with him for four years. The major was competing with a certain Stephen Douglas for the congressional seat; Lincoln's presence would help him free some time for his political activities. After four years with the major, Lincoln went to work for Stephen T. Logan, whom Judge David Davis—later a U.S. Supreme Court justice under Lincoln—judged "the greatest natural lawyer of his day."[25] It was Logan who wrote the document admitting Lincoln to the bar. Through him Lincoln started to become more detail oriented and thorough, studying the law more closely, and thus becoming able to understand and foresee the adversary's moves. The firm practically dealt with all the cases that reached the Illinois Supreme Court. The lucky exposure made Lincoln one of the most successful lawyers by the time he left for Washington. By then he had brought some three hundred cases to the Illinois high court.

Before leaving the bar for the presidency, Lincoln partnered with William Herndon, not the logically expected step to take after Logan and Todd Stuart, since Herndon was inexperienced. Some believe that Herndon may have been a choice with political aims in mind, since his partner was a leader in the populist element of the Whigs, and Lincoln's marriage to Mary Todd singled him out as part of the aristocratic element of the party. Lincoln got on so well with Herndon that there never was any conflict in spite of their great differences. Herndon was nine years younger and a radical, while Lincoln in many respects was a conservative. Lincoln called his partner colloquially Billy, the other reverentially Mr. Lincoln. The two divided their fees, as Lincoln would remember, "down the middle." Lincoln did not drink; Herndon all too much. Herndon stated many years later with surprise that Lincoln never brought up his weakness with the bottle, except once when their collaboration came to an end.

Lincoln's district of law was the Eighth Circuit, which stretched over eleven thousand square miles. Lincoln rode along the circuit in a very simple buggy that traveled some four miles per hour along very poor roads. And it would take some ten weeks or more to finish riding the circuit. This way he got to know people of the law and personally meet potential future voters. He acquired a great reputation for integrity and fairness, gaining him the moniker of "honest Old Abe."

---

[25] Albert A. Woldman, *Lawyer Lincoln*, 39.

Lincoln and the Law: A Turning Point

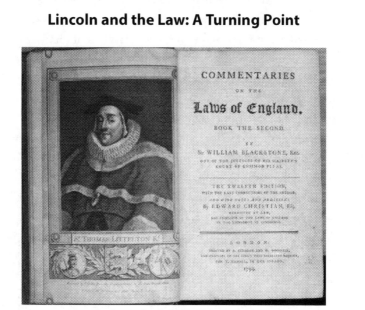

Credit: Trafford Publishing, UK, Ltd.

"One day a man who was migrating to the West drove up in front of my store with a wagon which contained his family and household plunder. He asked me if I would buy an old barrel for which he had no room in his wagon, and which contained nothing of special value" told Lincoln to Alban Jasper Conant who had painted his portrait in 1860. "I did not want it, but to oblige him I bought it, and paid him, I think, half a dollar for it. Without further examination I put it away in the store and forgot all about it. Some time after in overhauling things, I came upon the barrel and emptying it on the floor to see what it contained I found at the bottom of the rubbish pile a complete edition of Blackstone's Commentaries. I began to read those famous works, and I had plenty of time; for during the long summer days, when the farmers were busy with their crops, my customers were few and far between. . . . The more I read, the more intensely interested I became. Never in my whole life was my mind so thoroughly absorbed. I read until I devoured them."

From a conversation recorded by A. J. Conant in "My Acquaintance with Abraham Lincoln," in *Liber Scriptorum*, 172; *McClure's Magazine*, March 1909, 514. Other source in Albert A. Woldman, *Lawyer Lincoln* 15.

Lincoln's reputation for honesty was in fact so widespread that judges would ask him to sit in their stead—then a fairly common practice—when they were called away for some emergency. His clients hardly ever lost a case due to Lincoln's negligence, and he was also known to be fair to his opponents. He had great skill at cross-examining, such that the witnesses could rarely deceive or conceal. In what would turn out essential in the presidency, he knew the importance of avoiding confrontations, working out possible solutions for all, and mastering compromise. His philosophy could be summed up in his own words: "Persuade your neighbors to compromise whenever you can. Point out to them how the nominal winner is often a real loser—in fees, expenses, and waste of time. As a peacemaker the lawyer has a superior opportunity of being a good man."[26]

The young man probably studied the text of the Constitution in the early 1830s. Between the broad constructionism of Alexander Hamilton and the strict constructionism of Thomas Jefferson, Lincoln inclined to the latter. Where he departed from strict constructionism in particular was in the role of the government in supporting economic development, already in his support for Henry Clay's American System with its internal improvements and in relation to banking.

The range of interests represented by the young lawyer was truly astounding. Apart from individuals, Lincoln worked for banks, gas companies, insurance companies, and manufacturing and other commercial enterprises, but also for the interests that stood against them according to the cases. He was not their permanent representative, except for the Illinois Central Railroad.

Throughout his career Lincoln had the experience of lawyer, arbitrator/mediator, and judge, an all-around experience of the law; all of this in spite of the fact that a lawyer rarely makes a good judge. His competitors would invite him to be their associate or consulting counselor. Lincoln was also asked to be a special aide to local prosecutors in difficult cases or to substitute for attorneys when these were ill or absent. And towns would call on him to represent them as town solicitor to offer legal opinion or deal with litigation, not to mention to be an official examiner of applicants at the Illinois Bar.

---

[26] Brian R. Dirck, *Lincoln and the Constitution*, 9.

Lincoln was at his best when he had time to line up his arguments. He was most familiar with the deepest principles and the philosophy of the law, rather than with specific details of it. However, thanks to his prodigious memory, once he learned parts of the law, he would retain it. He also had a deep understanding of the human being; allied to it a capacity to leave aside the nonessential and focus on the essential principles.

Lincoln was at his best in cross-examining and at talking to the jury. He spoke the jurors' language and could give them the feeling that they were the ones trying the case. He had mastered the art of persuasion through deeply held inner conviction and thorough preparation. For this very reason he was not equally effective in all cases.

Lincoln was reputedly unconvincing when defending a man in the wrong. "No man was stronger than he when on the right side, and no man weaker on the opposite," observed lawyer and colleague Henry Whitney. While presenting the closing argument of a weak case, Whitney further reports, "the honesty of his mental processes forced him into a line of argument and admissions that were very damaging."[27]

However, Lincoln accepted all cases equally. He could not turn down a request from a slave-holder because he had too much respect for what the Constitution granted that person as a right. However, he could not plead for his client with conviction, and the ex-slaves were released. The client fled the state without paying his lawyer. This case would not have been very different from defending a murderer, which Lincoln also did.

Lincoln's recognized skills, plus his deep personal connections, created a connective tissue of lawyers and judges who appreciated him deeply and saw the potential for his nomination in the yet-to-be-born Republican Party. Unwittingly he had created a whole network of support, with Judge David Davis at its center. Together his friends campaigned for him and started creating the idea of Lincoln for president. They started to work out how to convince the party of his appeal with the masses and of his capacities. Judge Davis even stepped out from his profession to devote himself to campaigning for Lincoln full time and coordinate the whole campaign.

---

[27] Albert A. Woldman, *Lawyer Lincoln*, 193–194.

Head and Heart

Lincoln's childhood and youth were touched by the proximity of death. The first was that of his mother, followed by his sister Sarah and his brother Thomas. But no doubt the hardest one was that of Ann Rutledge, the daughter of a tavern owner, to whom he was engaged. In August 1835 Ann contracted "brain fever," probably typhoid, and died. Lincoln was devastated and deeply depressed for a time.

Those who knew Lincoln closely, especially Mary Todd, his future wife, realized how little of his feelings the young Lincoln would display. In fact, she reported that "when he felt most, he expressed the least."[28] He was awkward around women, up to freezing in their presence. No doubt the early experiences left a trace upon Lincoln, who would swing from complete self-confidence to discouragement and depression. He allied often opposing strains: sternness and tenderness, melancholic moods and playfulness, from effusive to serious and solemn.

Two things did help Lincoln, however. He could be easily distracted by what presented itself to him—a new situation, a social occasion, a friend's visit would move him from gloom to laughter. Witnesses would see him swing from the bottoms to the heights in a very short time. The second was humor, his constant tonic; he knew it had a therapeutic effect on his moodiness. But sometimes it could unleash its own problems.

Another outlet was his writing. In 1844, revisiting an area of Indiana close to where he had spent his youth, Lincoln wrote the poems we mentioned earlier. He felt that he could now complete the process of grieving for his mother. His emotions had been brought to the surface, and he had expressed them in verses. He relieved not only his grief but also his fear of madness. At that time he confronted the insanity that had taken hold of his friend Matthew Gentry.

One could say Lincoln was undergoing a test between passion and reason that would occupy him for some years and shape the person he would become. It appeared most clearly in his close relationships, most of all Mary Owens and Mary Todd, his future wife.

---

[28] David Herbert Donald, *Lincoln*, 98.

Mary Owens

With Mary Owens Lincoln went through a roller-coaster of emotions. His interest had been mixed with doubt about their lifestyle compatibility. He first put some distance from her, then offered a dispirited marriage proposal. When she refused, it was Lincoln who felt most hurt.

While he was under stress for the heartbreak, Lincoln did something uncharacteristic. In the Sangamon County courthouse he had an argument with attorney Jesse B. Thomas, deriding him and bringing him to tears by imitating very effectively his voice and gestures. However, Lincoln did not fail to apologize.[29]

Mary Todd

The courtship with Mary Todd brought together so many aspects of the young Lincoln and his personal growth. Mary was the pampered offspring of slaveholder aristocracy. She had received the best of schooling and had become a refined and graceful young woman, though others, like Bill Herndon, would find her haughty and sarcastic. It was her assurance and verve that charmed young Lincoln, as it had Stephen Douglas, with whom she had ostensibly flirted previously.

Mary and Abraham had a lot to share: their Kentucky roots, the Whig affiliation for which Mary was uncharacteristically vocal for women of her time, the love of poetry. Lincoln got as far as engagement before having once more cold feet. Again he feared he would not be able to offer Mary the lifestyle to which she was accustomed.

Assailed by strong emotions and self-doubt, he broke off with Mary, which was devastating to both of them. His depression lasted a whole week, and Lincoln got in touch with his hypochondriac nature. The two could not have found a way to mend were it not for others in their entourage who understood their plight. And politics and humor were part of the mix as well in unusual ways.

After the 1842 failure of the Bank of Illinois, dear to the Whigs, Lincoln attacked a Democratic state auditor, James Shields, under the disguise of the pen name Rebecca in the *Sangamon Journal*. In her column Rebecca, a simple but resourceful and outspoken countrywoman, poured sarcasm

---

[29] Roy Morris Jr., *The Long Pursuit: Abraham Lincoln's Thirty-Year Struggle with Stephen Douglas for the Heart and Soul of America*, 24.

on Shields and the local Democrats. Mary Todd took part in the ploy, with another woman. When an irate Shields pressed the journal to reveal the identity of Rebecca, Lincoln chivalrously decided to take the fall, and Shields challenged him to a duel.

Humor was leading to tragicomedy, and young Abraham could not find a way to extricate himself. Duels were illegal in Illinois, so it was arranged that the two would fight it off in nearby Alton, Missouri. The mounting farce was resolved thanks to the providential intervention of Dr. R. W. English and John J. Hardin, a Whig and relative of Mary Todd. Both parties were no doubt relieved. Lincoln was experiencing the devastating effects of his emotional instability when allied with a corrosive humor. He saw, as no one else could, the double-edged sword of the word.

In the last similar episode, Lincoln engaged against Van Buren, the Democratic presidential candidate, by helping to create the *Old Soldier*, a publication that carried "Lincoln speeches and Tippecanoe Almanacs" from the *Sangamon Journal*. In one speech Lincoln, without much scruple or evidence, accused Van Buren of discriminating in favor of free Black people at the expense of poor white people in matter of property rights.[30]

Here was a young man under the whim of the Mars forces, expressing themselves in word and deed, and allied for better or worse with the Mercury forces of satire and humor. The mix of the two was causing mischief in private and public life. The quest for balance between passion and reason occupied the young Lincoln both in his personal life and in his political career. What lived in this soul tension is also what he tried to address in American society, without failing, no doubt, to see the parallels. The integration of passion and reason formed a central place in Lincoln's politics and in his estimate of the rule of law.

Lincoln between Emotion and Reason

In 1838 in an address given to the Young Men's Lyceum—"The Perpetuation of Our Political Institutions"—Lincoln singled out political hyperemotionalism as a danger to American institutions, and advanced the need to resort to "the solid quarry of sober reason." He was referring to

---

[30] Roy Morris Jr., *The Long Pursuit: Abraham Lincoln's Thirty-Year Struggle with Stephen Douglas for the Heart and Soul of America*, 24.

outbreaks of mob violence and lynching of criminals, gamblers, abolitionists, and Black people. He called his fellow citizens to uphold the respect of law and appealed to "reason, cold, calculated, unimpassioned reason." The same emotionalism kept Lincoln at arm's length from the temperance movement. Not without passion he invoked reason thus: "Happy day, when, all appetites controlled, all passions subdued, . . . mind, all conquering mind, shall live and move the monarch of the world. Glorious consummation! Hail fall of Fury! Reign of Reason, all hail!"[31]

We can surmise that this stand for reason and against passion reflected his own stage of growth and his desire to curb his temper, which could on occasion flare up and bring him to dare his opponents to fistfights.

We can measure the progress by comparing these early episodes with the record of the future president. Later in life he showed a great mastery over his emotions and would hardly ever lose his temper.

In Lincoln's individuality we can surmise the reembodiment of someone of the Middle Ages or culture of Chartres, such was his striving to render concrete the knowledge of the seven liberal arts, no matter how remote a situation this was from the life of an uneducated frontier man.

The classical seven liberal arts included Grammatica, Dialectica, Rhetorica, forming the *Trivium*, and Arithmetica, Geometria, Astronomia, and Musica, forming the *Quadrivium*. We could say that the first part concerned the humanities, the second one the sciences. These disciplines of knowledge were at the time living experiences conveyed by living goddesses, divine-spiritual beings. In Steiner's words, the teachings that took place in the School of Chartres "contained the teachings from the old seership of the pre-Platonic Mysteries that had been imbued ever since with the contents of Christianity."[32]

Lincoln's connection with the Trivium appears in his love for the word. Through grammar he acquired the grasp of correct speech; dialectic/logic provided him with the framework of right thinking. Rhetoric, in which he excelled, built upon the two previous arts to create such art forms that could be remembered by others.

---

[31] Abraham Lincoln's Temperance Address of 1842.
[32] Rudolf Steiner, *Karmic Relationships*, Volume 3, lecture of July 13, 1924.

Lincoln did not achieve the complete Quadrivium formation. He still yearned for this scientific integration, as we can see in his efforts to unite science and faith, which continued up to his death. He also showed it in his love for Thales's geometry treatises, for understanding evolution, and, in his spare time, with the invention he patented.

Karmic Themes

Illinois reunited some dense karmic threads in the time leading to the Civil War. Lincoln's early legal career brought him into connection with Stephen T. Logan. In his office worked four future U.S. senators and three governors of states.[33] The 1836–37 Illinois legislature included one future president of the United States, one presidential contender, five future federal senators, seven future federal representatives, one governor, and three generals.[34]

Both lawyer/politicians adopted Illinois as their home state after immigrating there. Lincoln came from Kentucky, a slave state. Stephen Douglas who came from Vermont had not known slavery; he came closer to it, however, through marriage and political choices. The two present one stark contrast after the other; a leitmotif of polarities piles up at every possible level.

Douglas was the son of a physician of a long-established Vermont family with links to Revolutionary days. His paternal grandfather had served five terms in the Vermont General Assembly. His father died when Douglas was two, and the family fell from fortune. Douglas apprenticed with a Vermont cabinetmaker, but quit after eight months. He first moved to Cleveland, then to St. Louis, and finally west-central Illinois, where Lincoln had arrived four years earlier.

Like Lincoln, Douglas soon became interested in the political debate, siding with the Jackson Democrats from age fifteen. As Lincoln fixed his allegiance to Whig politics immediately, so Douglas recalls, "From this moment [fixing his attention on Jackson], my politics became fixed, and all

---

[33] Albert A. Woldman, *Lawyer Lincoln*, 39.
[34] Roy Morris Jr., *The Long Pursuit: Abraham Lincoln's Thirty-Year Struggle with Stephen Douglas for the Heart and Soul of America*, 17.

subsequent reading, reflection and observation have but confirmed my early attachment to the cause of Democracy."[35]

The two rivals contrasted in more than one way. Lincoln was detached and rational, moreover, abstemious; Douglas loved alcohol, women, and cigars. He was an impulsive fighter. And nothing could contrast more than the physical appearance of the two lawyers.

As Lincoln was tall and lanky, so was Douglas unusually short with a massive head. His abundant dark hair and flashing eyes, his aggressive, combative, defiant attitude was accompanied with great resources of energy, self-confidence, and audacity. Always impeccably dressed, he was a renowned and feared orator with great ease in language, attacking his opponents with force and vehemence. He could be evasive when convenient, but able to charm or please his audience, knowing what their prejudices were and willing to exploit them. All of these qualities earned him the moniker "little giant." Already in the early 1830s, his personal impulsiveness drove Douglas to extremes, such as the caning of the journalist Simeon Francis for something he had said that had incensed Douglas's pride.[36]

It seems that Lincoln and Douglas first met in 1834, but nothing worth noting emerged from the early days. Douglas was working on behalf of John Wyatt, a Democratic legislator. Like Lincoln he was an itinerant attorney, for the First Judicial District covering eight counties, among which was Lincoln's Sangamon. The two started gaining a reputation, though in different ways. An apparently popular judgment in Illinois was that "With a good case, Lincoln is the best lawyer in the State, but in a bad case, Douglas is the best lawyer the State can produce."[37]

Already Douglas's ambition was aiming much higher. He found an outlet in organizing what was practically the first American political convention for the Democrats in December 1835. With the popularity and reputation he gained, he easily was elected to office in his district in 1836, at age twenty-three. In the same year Douglas had also been awarded the appointment of registrar of the Springfield Land Office, a political reward for helping the election of President Van Buren. From this he derived an additional income of three thousand dollars in interests and fees.

---

[35] Roy Morris Jr., *The Long Pursuit*, 10.

[36] Roy Morris Jr., *The Long Pursuit*, 26.

[37] Albert A. Woldman, *Lawyer Lincoln*, 257.

Thanks to his political organizing skills, Douglas was nominated for Congress to replace the Democrat William L. May, who had fallen in political disgrace. Interestingly Douglas and Lincoln confronted each other in court on a murder case, which had links to Douglas's nomination for Congress, the deposition of William May from Congress having been the motivation for the murder. Lincoln won the case that led to the acquittal of the presumed murderer, and Douglas was defeated by a narrow margin.[38]

The paths of the political contenders started intertwining more and more. Having become the leaders of Whig and Democratic youths respectively, they debated each other in 1839 for three days, especially around the issue of the national bank, opposed by the Van Buren Democrats. Lincoln was keenly aware of having been defeated by his rival and of failing to promote the view of the national bank.

Douglas continued to ascend the political ladder at vertiginous speed. After the Democrat Harrison's victory for the presidency, the young politician became the Illinois Secretary of State at the unprecedented age of twenty-seven. Not content with this achievement, he also filled a vacant seat on the Illinois Supreme Court, to which Lincoln had opportunity to present cases. Two years later Douglas was elected to the U.S. Senate, while Lincoln lost his congressional seat and returned to the practice of the law and to his new wife Mary Todd, another interesting mutual connection and rivalry of the two ambitious politicians.

It is true that Douglas faced the handicap of Mary's entrenched personal and family Whig loyalties. Douglas and Mary flirted publicly for a while, but Mary later told a friend that she had turned down his offer for marriage. In a striking manner, while still in Kentucky, Mary had often joked that "she intended to marry a man who would some day become President of the United States."[39] The lucky choice rewarded her between the two contenders.

Douglas married instead Martha Martin of South Carolina, soon inheriting a 20% commission on all profits of a 2,500-acre cotton plantation in Mississippi with some one hundred and fifty slaves as part of it. This

---

[38] Roy Morris Jr., *The Long Pursuit*, 21.

[39] David Herbert Donald, *Lincoln*, 85.

caused him no doubt some political embarrassment, but earned him political capital with the South.

By the end of the 1850s Douglas's career had been one of success after success; that of Lincoln alternated some success with many failures. In the winter of 1855–56 Lincoln reminisced in writing: "We were both young men; he a trifle younger than me [Lincoln was 4 years older]. Even then we were very ambitious; I, perhaps, quite as much as he. With me the race of ambition has been a failure—a flat failure; with him it has been a splendid success. His name fills the nation; and is not unknown, even, in foreign lands."[40] While Lincoln had returned to anonymity in Illinois, Douglas was becoming the most powerful member of the U.S. Senate.

Even though retired from public office, and maybe unbeknownst to himself, Lincoln had accumulated considerable political and human capital, which offers us indications, however vague, of his karmic connections. In his profession he gained the reputation that led to his nickname "Honest Abe" or "Honest Old Abe." Here the "old" did not carry a direct relationship to age. Later on people in his White House entourage called him "the Ancient One" because of his seasoned wisdom. This aura of respect was also tenderly reflected by Lincoln's associate of twenty-three years, Bill Herndon, who could never depart from calling his elder Mr. Lincoln. It seems unconscious inklings pointed to Lincoln's hidden and deeper stature, his seasoned karmic being.

The Issue of Slavery

Of great interest are also Lincoln's early positions on slavery. On his journey down the Mississippi to New Orleans, Lincoln had been exposed to the reality of slavery. Though the issue could hardly be approached without completely losing considerable political capital, from the very beginning Lincoln pronounced himself against it, saying, for example, "Although volume upon volume is written to prove slavery a good thing, we never hear of the man who wishes to take the good of it, by being a slave himself."[41]

Lincoln the thinker was framing the issue with growing precision and courage. He argued he was "naturally anti-slavery" just as his father before him, but he felt himself bound to respecting the Constitution in fighting

---

[40] Roy Morris Jr., *The Long* Pursuit, 1.
[41] Brian R. Dirck, *Lincoln and the Constitution*, 12.

LUIGI MORELLI

against slavery, only as it concerned its extension. "I hold it to be a paramount duty of us in the free states, due to the Union of the States, and perhaps to liberty itself (paradox though it may seem) to let the slavery of the other states alone; while, on the other hand, I hold it to be equally clear, that we should never knowingly lend ourselves directly or indirectly, to prevent that slavery from dying a natural death."[42]

In line with his early concerns, he voted for the Wilmot Proviso though he did not actively promote it. And he found the matter of slavery in Washington, D.C., to be a matter of national embarrassment in front of all foreigners, although he believed slavery could only be ended there with the consent of the people. He proposed a referendum in which all white males could decide on the matter and slaves would be paid their full value to masters who agreed to sell them. To this end he had worked behind the scenes to craft a compromise that the South could accept. However, once the plan was publicized, all support vanished and Lincoln didn't introduced the bill.

Lincoln distanced himself both from the racism of his milieu and from views that, although generous and well meaning, ran afoul of the reality of the American Constitution and the law of the land.

Though retired from politics, Lincoln's mind followed very closely the fate of the nation. When he finally returned to politics on the verge of the Civil War, his chance of success seemed slim at best, but not so for everybody. In April 1860 Douglas and Lincoln were invited to dine at the residence of Isaac N. Arnold; someone, drunk with enthusiasm, proposed a toast: "May Illinois furnish the next president."[43] The same was presaged in the negative by Lincoln in the years leading to his presidency. Circuit lawyers, often his travel companions, noticed in Lincoln an unpredictable moodiness. A certain Henry Clay Whitney, who shared rooms with him, remembered that his friend had nightmares during which "he was talking the wildest and most incoherent nonsense all to himself."[44] Closer to him, Herndon recorded Lincoln's complaint "that he had done nothing to make any human being remember that he had lived."[45]

[42] David Herbert Donald, *Lincoln*, 134.
[43] Douglas L. Wilson, *Lincoln's Sword: The Presidency and the Power of Words*, 189.
[44] David Herbert Donald, *Lincoln*, 163.
[45] David Herbert Donald, *Lincoln*, 81.

46

Chapter 3
Prelude to the Civil War

LINCOLN'S LIFE WAS FRAMED WITHIN the years in which took place a certain acceleration in the tensions leading to the Civil War. From 1812 to 1820—from the time Lincoln was three to eleven—the Union admitted three new slave states (Louisiana, Mississippi, Alabama) thereby significantly altering the delicate balance of power between North and South so fragilely enshrined in the Constitution.

All slave or all free states seemed to be the unescapable logic set to take hold of the nation. Lincoln did not come to his political career unprepared on this issue. Already in his youth some inner stirrings had informed him of how much weight the issue held in the scales of justice.

In his debates with Stephen Douglas, he would be quite explicit:

> I hate [indifference to slavery] because of the monstrous injustice of slavery itself. I hate it because it deprives our republican example of its just influence in the world, enables the enemies of free institutions, with plausibility, to taunt us as hypocrites, causes the real friends of freedom to doubt our sincerity, and especially because it forces so many really good men amongst ourselves into an open war with the very fundamental principles of civil liberty-criticizing the Declaration of Independence, and insisting that there is no right principle of action but self-interest.[46]

---

[46] Speech at Peoria, IL, on October 15, 1854.

Lincoln could not speak for racial equality, which few Northerners were ready to accept. Nevertheless he had the courage to state that "there is no reason in the world why the negro is not entitled to all the natural rights enumerated in the Declaration of Independence, the right to life, liberty and the pursuit of happiness." He perceived of his adversaries, "If they would repress all tendencies to liberty and ultimate emancipation . . . they must penetrate the human soul and eradicate the love of liberty."[47]

However, other considerations overrode Lincoln's deeper feelings on the issue. His respect for the Constitution did not allow Lincoln the lawyer to invoke an abstract, personal higher ground rather than the concrete compact that in effect bound the nation together. He was ready to respect all laws concerning slavery including the fugitive slave laws; witness the fact that he did serve at least one slaveholder as a client.

Having studied the history of the Constitution, Lincoln cogently argued that at least twenty-one of the thirty-nine founders demonstrated by their votes that the government had power to control slavery in the national territories. And some others were clearly on this side of the issue, though they were not called to vote on it (e.g., Benjamin Franklin, Gouverneur Morris, and Alexander Hamilton).[48] In other words Lincoln believed that the Founding Fathers had operated in such a way as to contain slavery and make it fade over time, this perhaps naively.

Now it was this very wish that was threatened. If the Southern slaveholders were to have their way, they were going to rewrite history to support their positions. And this was in fact their intention; slavery was no longer held as a necessary evil, but as a positive good. From the early 1800s a new narrative arose. It may have first been expressed by Robert Walsh in 1819: "The physical condition of the American Negro is on the whole, not comparatively alone, but positively good, and he is exempt from those racking anxieties—the exacerbates of despair, to which the English manufacturer and peasant are subject to in the pursuit of their pittance."[49] On the economic and political fronts, event after event had led to a radicalization and polarization. We will look at the economy first.

---

[47] Speech at Columbus, September 16, 1859.

[48] David Herbert Donald, *Lincoln*, 238.

[49] https://wiki2.org/en/Slavery_as_a_positive_good_in_the_United_States

North and South: The Economy

In great part because of slavery, there was a larger issue affecting the delicate equilibrium between North and South. The northeast controlled the nation's manufacturing and was its financial and trading center. The northwest produced the nation's wheat and livestock; the South relied mostly on cotton. The disastrous reliance on monoculture that plantation-based cotton production generated tended to exhaust the land, and the slaveholding elite felt the pressure to expand their holdings to assure future financial viability.

The South continued to import most of its manufactured goods from the North or from Europe, especially Great Britain. And both markets provided an outlet for the exportation of cotton. Because manufactured goods were cheaper in Europe, even after cost of transportation, the South found it more advantageous to privilege this route of trade. National policy altered this delicate economic balance by setting duties on manufactured items that competed with Northern industry. Europe reacted by discontinuing the purchase of American cotton. Thus the South was hurt twice, while by the same token Northern industry lost the incentive to compete and meet the demand at lower costs. Added to this was the fear raised by abolitionism in the whole of the South, considering that a fugitive slave would entail the loss of about $ 1,500 each, a very high cost at the time. Even though some were considering moving from enslaved to hired labor, economic pressure made this move more difficult by the day and tied them to the inherited economic institution of slavery.[50]

Already the Tariff of 1828 had been dubbed the Tariff of Abominations by the Southern opponents, and South Carolina felt justified in passing the Ordinance of Nullification, declaring the tariff void because it threatened the state's economic interests. Although at this point no other state had followed their example, in light of the outcry, the tariff was revised in 1832 and in 1833 thanks to the conciliatory efforts of Henry Clay, offering the South some relief.

---

[50] G. Edward Griffin, *The Creature of Jekyll Island*, 372.

North and South: Politics

Due to the pressure of the expansion of slavery through the new states entering the Union, Henry Clay promoted the Missouri Compromise, which was adopted by Congress in 1820. In the effort to preserve the balance between slave and free states, it admitted Missouri as a slave state and prohibited slavery in all new territories west of the Mississippi River and north of 36°30' latitude.

Another step, or rather divisive attempt, came with the Wilmot Proviso of 1846. It showed how polarizing the issue of slave versus free states had become. The measure was devised for preventing slavery in the territory captured from Mexico, an area south of what had been agreed upon by the Missouri Compromise. The Northern electorate resented the political power of slaveholders in Congress, whom they equated to a growing oligarchic power. The measure passed a number of times in the House. It never became law, having been blocked in the Senate by Southern senators, but it considerably increased animosity between North and South.

Consider that even in the South few believed possible the extension of slavery in the new territories. Even when New Mexico, Utah, and Kansas were opened to slavery, there was a comparatively small emigration of slaveholders. The very radical Calhoun himself doubted that slavery could be extended to the territories conquered from Mexico. The issue had become largely symbolic. What individuals thought privately was not mirrored at the political level, where every new issue increased polarization.

The universal Southern opposition to the Wilmot Proviso became a rallying cry and symbol for Southern equality in the nation. Although the vote on the proviso went mostly along sectional lines, not party lines, Stephen Douglas found himself in a difficult position. He and only three other Northern Democrats voted against it. He tried to work another compromise barring slavery from the Oregon Territory, but his decision marked him as a traitor in the eyes of the abolitionists.

Soon after Douglas found himself embracing the concept of popular sovereignty in its application to the slavery matter. It devolved to the residents of new territories the ability to vote on whether slavery should be allowed, removing this decision from federal jurisdiction.

The so-called Compromise of 1850 stipulated that California would be admitted as a free state, and the remaining new land conceded by Mexico would be subdivided into the New Mexico and Utah territories. The states formed within the new territories would decide on the matter of slavery by applying the concept of popular sovereignty. In exchange for banning the slave trade in Washington, DC, the Fugitive Slave Law would be applied more stringently.

Though he still hoped to avoid the repeal of the 1850 Compromise, in 1854 Douglas drafted the Kansas–Nebraska Act. In so doing he further moved toward the adoption of popular sovereignty in the Nebraska territory to replace the previous prohibition of slavery. Dropping the Missouri Compromise of 1820, which did not allow slavery in Kansas, was a major victory for the slaveholder interests. Because of the introduction of popular sovereignty, pro- and antislavery settlers moved into Kansas with the intention of determining the future of the state. It led to the equivalent of a state civil war, known as Bleeding Kansas. Antislavery forces across the North rallied into a movement that led to the emergence of the Republican Party, committed to stopping the expansion of slavery.

Stephen Douglas was what one could call a political horse trader with little patience for principles. He interpreted the Constitution in a flexible way, as allowing the majority to produce changes, even in matters that should have involved judicial review. And Douglas needed Southerners in order to reach the presidency.

At this point Lincoln, spurred by national events, decided to run again for the federal legislature. And one of his first steps was to call Douglas to publicly debate with him. He tried for several weeks; Douglas, visibly reluctant, had to concede. The first debate took place on October 4, 1854. This was improvised by Lincoln who had listened to Douglas defend the Kansas-Nebraska Act for three hours the previous day. Lincoln debated popular sovereignty and its lawfulness. He harkened back to the Declaration of Independence and pointed to the inconsistency of popular sovereignty with this illustrious precedent. Lincoln's speech received great applause.

In wanting to return to public office, Lincoln saw that the issue of slavery's legality was affecting all aspects of American policy. Slavery was contrasting with the vision of free enterprise that Lincoln espoused. Moreover, he saw in popular sovereignty an abdication of the powers of Congress over the territories. Not to mention that now slaveholders could make the Three-Fifths

Clause play in their favor. Moreover, a citizen of a free state could make himself slaveholder in a new territory. And the events kept accelerating.

There were many more issues at stake that escaped immediate scrutiny. Most Western nations but the U.S. had by then abandoned slavery. The issue made friends of America doubt its claims and principles.

Supreme Court Decisions

On March 6, 1857, the Supreme Court decided the *Dred Scott* case, in which a enslaved man in Missouri had been taken by his owner to Illinois, then to the territory of Minnesota. When his owner died, Scott claimed his freedom, but was denied on the ground of not being a U.S. citizen. Chief Justice Roger B. Taney, a Democrat and a slaveholder, argued that congressional enactments that excluded slavery from the national territories were "not warranted by the Constitution." And he added that neither the Constitution nor the Declaration of Independence were intended to include Black people. This set off massive dissent in the North.

Taney wanted to exclude African Americans from every notion of rights and citizenship, and show that they were held as inferior race at the time of the writing of the Constitution. Chief Justice Taney would have extended this criterium even to emancipated black people. He explicitly stated that Black people were not included in the Declaration of Independence preamble. Taney emphasized the rights of property, wanting to treat the African American completely from this perspective. His fervor enthused Southern slaveholders who were feeling they were been given future guarantees against any future inroads against slavery. Lincoln knew that Taney wanted to divorce the Constitution from all organic links with the Declaration of Independence.

The lines were drawn when Stephen Douglas explicitly endorsed the *Dred Scott* decision of the Court, even though it stood at odds with popular sovereignty, since it stated that no government legislation could place limits on slavery. In addition, the case of *Lemmon vs The People* that considered the right of a Virginia slaveholder to bring his enslaved people to the state of New York in transit to Texas was making its way to the Supreme Court. It was likely that the Court was going to rule in the same direction as *Dred Scott*.

What Justice Roger Taney Said

The following are some of the assertions of Roger Taney, as a justice and a private citizen, which give us an idea of what stood at stake under his tenure on the Supreme Court:

"We think ... that [black people] are not included, and were not intended to be included, under the word 'citizens' in the Constitution, and can therefore claim none of the rights and privileges which that instrument provides for and secures to citizens of the United States. On the contrary, they were at that time [of America's founding] considered as a subordinate and inferior class of beings who had been subjugated by the dominant race, and, whether emancipated or not, yet remained subject to their authority, and had no rights or privileges but such as those who held the power and the Government might choose to grant them." —Dred Scott, 60 U.S. at 404–05.

Justice Taney, reviewing laws from the original American states that involved the status of black Americans at the time of the Constitution's drafting in 1787, concluded that these laws showed that a "perpetual and impassable barrier was intended to be erected between the white race and the one which they had reduced to slavery."

"Now, ... the right of property in a slave is distinctly and expressly affirmed in the Constitution. . . . Upon these considerations, it is the opinion of the court that the act of Congress which prohibited a citizen from holding and owning property of this kind in the territory of the United States north of the [36°N 36' latitude] line therein mentioned, is not warranted by the Constitution, and is therefore void." Dred Scott, 60 U.S. at 451–52.

"What Dred Scott's master might lawfully do with Dred Scott, in the free state of Illinois, every other master may lawfully do with any other one, or 1,000 slaves, in Illinois, or in any other free state."

"Every intelligent person whose life has been passed in a slaveholding State, and who has carefully observed the character and capacity of the African race, will see that a general and sudden emancipation would be absolute ruin to the Negroes, as well as to the white population."

"Thank God that at least in one place, all men are equal: in the church of God. I do not consider it any degradation to kneel side by side with a Negro in the house of our Heavenly Father."

Lincoln's Return to Politics

On the wake of the *Dred Scott* decision, Douglas returned to Illinois now armed with the idea of Black people as an inferior race, accusing Lincoln and the Republicans of wanting to amalgamate the races.

Lincoln knew that few Northerners were ready to accept full racial equality. Nevertheless he had the courage to state that "there is no reason in the world why the negro is not entitled to all the natural rights enumerated in the Declaration of Independence, the right to life, liberty and the pursuit of happiness."

Lincoln started focusing on the legal aspects of the *Dred Scott* decision. He could apply all his legal expertise and skills in explaining it to the average citizen. In his *House Divided* speech of June 16, 1858, he announced that America would turn either all slave or all free. Deploring the influence of the Kansas-Nebraska Act, he went on to utter prophetic statements:

> It [agitation caused by that policy] will not cease, until a crisis shall have been reached, and passed. A house divided against itself cannot stand. I believe this government cannot endure, permanently half slave and half free. I do not expect the Union to be dissolved—I do not expect the house to fall—but I do expect that it will cease to be divided. It will become all one thing or all the other. Either the opponents of slavery, will . . . place it where the public mind shall rest in the belief that it is in the course of ultimate extinction; or its advocates will put it forward, till it shall become alike lawful in all the States, old as well as new—North as well as South.

That he was not hyperbolizing can be confirmed by slavery apologists like George Fitzhugh who were arguing that the United States had to become all free or all slave.[51]

The imagery in the speech had a profound effect on the nation. Lincoln captured the essence of the dilemma further: "If any man choose

---

[51] David Herbert Donald, *Lincoln*, 207.

to enslave another, no third man shall be allowed to object." In the speech Lincoln already attacked the effect of *Dred Scott* on Douglas's popular sovereignty.

The 1858 Illinois Republican convention, held in Springfield, chose Lincoln as its candidate for U.S. senator to oppose Douglas. After giving his *House Divided* speech, Lincoln set for the party the work of opposing slavery. At the end of July Lincoln wrote to Douglas, asking him to share time in addressing the same audiences that the senator had planned to address. Douglas agreed setting the stage for the seven now famous Lincoln-Douglas debates.

Armed with his inescapable logic, Lincoln wanted to confront Douglas and corner him with the Illinois voters, but most of all with the nation. He knew he could prove that the *Dred Scott* decision constituted a threat for the whole nation, that it was part of a conscious attempt to extend slavery. He knew that *Dred Scott* was the weakness in Douglas's armor. He would try to deny the inescapable conclusions of the decision.

Lincoln knew that Douglas would have to answer the question about *Dred Scott* in a way that would please Illinois voters but alienate his support from the South, and he drove him relentlessly to the corner. Lincoln pointed out that Douglas was taking a way out by predicating that "[slavery] may lawfully be driven away from a place where it has a lawful right to be," thus treating lightly the decisions of the Supreme Court. This was Lincoln the cross-examiner, at his best.

In the debate Lincoln was appealing to reason; Douglas could only counter by leveraging his audience's emotions (see box: Quotes from the Lincoln-Douglas Debates). In the end it was a sort of stalemate between the two. Even Lincoln's supporters at times questioned his choices and strategy. After the debates Lincoln won the majority of the votes, but not the majority of the districts; Douglas was elected, capturing 54 seats in the legislature against Lincoln's 46.

Quotes from the Lincoln-Douglas Debates

The following, short quotes give a feeling of the tenor of the debates and tactics of the candidates:

Why can [the nation] not exist divided into free and slave States? Washington, Jefferson, Franklin, Madison, Hamilton, Jay . . . made this Government divided into free States and slave States. (Douglas)

My understanding is that Popular Sovereignty, as now applied to the question of slavery, does allow the people of a Territory to have slavery if they want to, but does not allow them not to have it if they do not want it. (Lincoln)

If you desire negro citizenship, if you desire to allow them to come into the State and settle with the white man, if you desire them to vote on an equality with yourselves, and to make them eligible to office, to serve on juries, and to adjudge your rights, then support Mr. Lincoln and the Black Republican party, who are in favor of the citizenship of the negro. (Douglas)

I agree with Judge Douglas [the black man] is not my equal in many respects—certainly not in color, perhaps not in moral or intellectual endowment. But in the right to eat the bread, without leave of anybody else, which his own hand earns, he is my equal and the equal of Judge Douglas, and the equal of every living man. (Lincoln)

Do you desire to turn this beautiful State into a free negro colony, in order that when Missouri abolishes slavery she can send one hundred thousand emancipated slaves into Illinois, to become citizens and voters, on an equality with yourselves? (Douglas)

When they remind us of their constitutional rights, I acknowledge them, not grudgingly, but fully, and fairly; and I would give them any legislation for the reclaiming of their fugitives, which should not, in its stringency, be more likely to carry a free man into slavery, than our ordinary criminal laws are to hang an innocent one. (Lincoln)

The Abolitionists are all for him, Lovejoy and Farnsworth are canvassing for him, Giddings is ready to come here in his behalf, and the negro speakers are already on the stump for him. (Douglas)

On the other hand, the effect was the reverse on the national scene. Lincoln acquired larger notoriety with his reprinted speeches; Douglas suffered an irreversible blow when the Democratic Party fractured along sectional lines. The words of Louisiana's Senator Judah P. Benjamin, indicting Douglas, spoke for many in the South: "We accuse him for this . . . that he would act under the decision [*Dred Scott*] and consider it a doctrine of the party; that having said that to us here in the Senate, he went home, and under the stress of a local election, his knees gave way; his whole person trembled. . . . the grand prize for his ambition today slips from his grasp because of his faltering in the former contest, and his success in the canvass for the Senate purchased for an ignoble price, has cost him the loss of the Presidency of the United States."[52] The senator was alluding to the rift in the Democratic Party. On May 3, 1860, Douglas was rejected by the South and became the candidate of the North; the Southern faction of the party opted for John C. Breckenridge.

Lincoln had sacrificed his short-term goals in view of a larger prize. Defeat apart, Lincoln was recognized as an essential promotor of the fledgling Republican Party, and thus was invited to give the closing speech at the party's organizing assembly in Bloomington, Indiana, in May. At this point Lincoln the politician was still very much subordinated to Lincoln the lawyer and constitutional expert. He still abided by the Fugitive Slave Act and was ready to concede on the extension of slavery if it allowed the survival of the Union.

Republican Candidate and President

Having become the leading Republican figure in Illinois, Lincoln took it upon himself to preserve and strengthen a fragile coalition and an indebted party. He had to exert moral and intellectual leadership in facing ideological threats.

Douglas continued to be a formidable adversary. The consummate attorney had the ability to reconcile the most contradictory positions and reassure the voters he was on their side with his choices. The little giant was attempting to move toward an opportunistic center that would reject both

---

[52] David Herbert Donald, *Lincoln*, 269–270.

Northern and Southern radicals. Lincoln continued to offer speeches that criticized Douglas in continuation of the debates. He wanted to educate the electorate to realize that Douglas was pulling a smokescreen that prevented people from seeing that he was gradually undermining the resistance to the spread of slavery throughout the Union. In his 1859 speeches he alarmed his listeners to how "the mass of white men are really injured by the effect of slave labor in the vicinity of the fields of their own labor."[53]

Through the success of his speeches in Iowa, Indiana, Kentucky, and Kansas, Lincoln started to envision being a candidate. In the meantime the press started floating the idea. At this point Lincoln had both pros and cons. His major strength lay in his profound expertise in constitutional matters, and in the fact that he had created very few enemies. On the other hand he had a scant political track record: he had served one term in Washington but lost two senatorial races. To his advantage he did not have one single strong rival; all the competitors had strengths and flaws. The most prominent of them, William Seward, was perceived as an extremist by part of the electorate.

Lincoln bided his time and enlarged his appeal by republishing his 1858 speeches with Douglas, which together with other ones became an instant bestseller, just in time for the 1860 nominating convention. He continued in the same vein by delivering his famous Cooper Union address in which he skillfully mapped the futures open to the nation. He linked his position convincingly to constitutional and historical precedent. And he reaffirmed the Republicans' intention of confining slavery to its present territories, excluding it from others.

The Cooper Union speech had greatly increased Lincoln's popularity. On the wake of it, Noah Brooks of the *New York Tribune* went as far as comparing Lincoln to St Paul. The whole speech was reprinted by four New York papers and was used as a Republican tract in New York, Albany, Chicago, and Detroit papers.

Lincoln had played a conservative image to the electorate, that of one trying to preserve the legacy of the Founding Fathers. From New York Lincoln went to New England to seek to consolidate the connections with prominent Republicans. After this he did not hide from people close to him his desire to run for the presidency.

---

[53] David Herbert Donald, *Lincoln*, 233.

For political calculations, if the Democrats named Douglas, the Republicans would have to name someone from the West. Lincoln's fate was once again tied to that of Douglas. His greater strength was that no one objected to him, and he made sure not to step on anyone's toes.

Luck also played in the candidate's favor when Chicago was chosen over Saint Louis and brought the nomination convention close to Lincoln's home. Note that Chicago was chosen by one vote, the one cast by Judge Davis, the closest Lincoln collaborator.

At the Illinois State Convention Lincoln was conveniently presented as the "rail splitter," though that had been a minor part of Lincoln's earlier activities. Still, the image was fitting, making Lincoln the representative of the self-made man. His moderate views and unanimous Illinois support played fully to Lincoln's advantage.

After the first ballot Lincoln already emerged second to Seward, who did not secure a majority. After a second he was only three votes behind the seasoned politician. The third ballot brought him again to three votes short of the majority. Finally, the four Ohio representatives switched their votes from Salmon Chase to Lincoln, assuring him the majority. Fate had something even better in store. Soon after, the Democrat convention split into a Northern faction behind Douglas and a Southern one that nominated John C. Breckinridge. In the end the latter prevailed, sparing Lincoln the challenge of a much more insidious ideological challenge.

In the lead-up to the counting of votes and casting of electoral votes, Lincoln kept silence about his positions, other than reasserting his loyalty to constitutional principles. On February 22 he took advantage of the setting of Philadelphia's Independence Hall to reaffirm with emphasis his attachment to the Declaration of Independence: "If [the country] can't be saved upon that principle, it will be truly awful. . . . I was about to say I would rather be assassinated on this spot than to surrender it."

In his attachment to Constitution and Union, Lincoln was willing to make concessions, such as granting New Mexico the choice of being a slave state, if that meant no further extension of slavery in the national territories. He was ever more watchful that Republicans might fall prey to the perniciously seductive call of popular sovereignty, to which he was adamantly unwilling to yield.

The Looming Confrontation

If the national challenges were not enough to daunt a president with the limited powers entrusted to him by the U.S. Constitution, we should also consider that there were other limitations imposed by global politics.

The situation that Lincoln inherited as president of a divided country was keenly followed by America's competing powers. The real danger of the looming Civil War was the break-up of the union and the weakening of the resulting parts on the international scene to the advantage of France and England primarily, but also Spain.

German chancellor Otto von Bismarck perceived the situation thus:

> I know of absolute certainty that the division of the United States into federations of equal force was decided long before the Civil War by the high financial powers of Europe.... Of course, in the inner circle of finance the voice of the Rothschilds prevailed. They saw an opportunity for prodigious booty if they could substitute two feeble democracies, burdened with debt to financiers, . . . in place of a vigorous Republic sufficient unto herself. Therefore they sent emissaries into the field to exploit the question of slavery and to drive a wedge between the two parts of the Union.[54]

In a fractured political reality Lincoln and Breckenridge had received only 58% of all votes; Lincoln, whose name had not even been entered on the ballots of ten states, had 40% and a majority of the electoral vote.

Not long after Lincoln's success, the South started to stir. South Carolina was the first in calling a convention for December 10, 1860, in which the state would contemplate secession. The same was true for every state of the Deep South in the following month. Soon after South Carolina, Florida, Mississippi, Alabama, Georgia, Louisiana, and Texas delegations met in Montgomery, Alabama, to draft a constitution for the new Confederate States of America. This was to be followed by the seizure of federal arsenals,

---

[54] Ellen Hodgson Brown, *The Web of Debt*, 90.

the first occurring on January 9, when South Carolina troops fired on Fort Sumter.

Lincoln's administration contemplated a few options. One was the possibility of evacuating Fort Sumter while reinforcing other federal forts. When on April 12 the Confederates moved to attack Fort Sumter, the garrison was forced to surrender. Lincoln's strategy had paid off. He wanted his government to stand in the eyes of the world as the aggressed party. This allowed Lincoln not to declare war, and to stand as the preserver of the Union.

Lincoln's challenges had just begun. As he had shored up the fragile alliances of the Republican Party prior to the election, now he shrewdly reckoned with the new reality and the need to compromise and keep everybody happy. He had to accept working with his previous political rivals: Seward, Chase, Bates, and among the others, Dayton, Judd, Blair, and Welles. Not only were some of these his rivals; at times they were also bitter antagonists to each other. These various individuals, however, balanced out various constituencies and encompassed American geography, from the East to the Midwest, to border slave states.

Lincoln was playing a gamble of tremendous importance for the future of the United States. We could say, in echoing Martin Luther King, that he was "trying to find a way out of no way."

America at the Abyss

We know from Steiner's work that America offers a particular geography for the confrontation with what he called the "double":

> A short time before we are born we are permeated by another
> being; in our terminology we would call it an Ahrimanic
> spirit-being. This is within us just as our own soul is within
> us. These beings spend their life using human beings in
> order to be able to be in the sphere where they want to be.
> These beings have an extraordinarily high intelligence and
> a significantly developed will, but no warmth of heart at
> all, nothing of what we call human soul warmth (*Gemüt*).
> Thus we go through life in such a way that we have both our

souls and a double of this kind, who is much more clever, very much more clever than we are, who is very intelligent, but with a Mephistophelian intelligence, an Ahrimanic intelligence, and also an Ahrimanic will, a very strong will, a will that is much more akin to the nature-forces than our human will, which is regulated by the warmth of soul (*Gemüt*).[55]

The forces that have the greatest influence on this double, rising from below the earth, are strongest in some parts of the Earth than in others. This is the case where the magnetic forces work strongest because of the alignment of the mountains from north to south, as is the case in the Americas, most of all in the north.

This is the region of the earth where most of the mountain ranges run, not crosswise, from east to west, but where the ranges primarily run, from north to south (for this is also connected with these forces) where one is in the vicinity of the magnetic North Pole. This is the region where above all the kinship is developed with the Mephistophelian-Ahrimanic nature through outer conditions. And through this kinship much is brought about in the continuing evolution of the earth.[56]

The Ahrimanic beings that animate the double bring about an obliteration of the forces of the rhythmic system, an extinction of the heart forces. At the time preceding the fall of the spirits of darkness, while the battle of Michael took place in the spiritual world, roughly from 1841–42 to 1879, the United States were undergoing a battle for their soul. Ahriman was dictating the extension of a most callous view of the human being, with slavery at its center, which would have obliterated the American founding impulse, and the Michaelic culture upon which it was founded. The battle in

---

[55] Rudolf Steiner, "The Mystery of the Double: Geographic Medicine," St. Gallen, lecture of November 16, 1917.
[56] Rudolf Steiner, "The Mystery of the Double: Geographic Medicine," St. Gallen, lecture of November 16, 1917.

the spiritual world formed a watershed for humanity; humanity had crossed a threshold. Whereas up to that time human beings received support from their physical body through the elemental beings that inhabit it, from then onwards they must draw that strength directly from the spiritual world. This includes everything through which we shape our moral character.[57]

In the U.S. Lincoln, almost singlehandedly, formed a counterweight to this devastating impulse. What Steiner says of Emerson below—in referring to the work of the double and its link with geographic conditions—applies to Lincoln, his contemporary:

> It is only necessary to think of Emerson in order to know that nothing is intended here as characteristic of a people. But Emerson was a man of European education through and through. This simply shows the two opposite poles that are developing. Precisely under such influences as have been characterized today, people such as Emerson develop, who develop as they do because they confront the double with complete humanity. On the other hand, people are developing such as Woodrow Wilson, who is a mere sheath of the double, through whom the double himself works with special effectiveness. Such people are essentially actual embodiments of the geographic nature of America.[58]

What stood at stake was America's risk of falling into a deep materialism and sealing its future possibility of evolution toward a science of the spirit. Lincoln had "confronted his double with complete humanity." His deep spirituality, that we will discuss in the next chapters, formed a rampart against a complete Ahrimanization of culture and delayed the tendencies that have brought this to pass in modern times.

The above, extreme reality, strengthening the double, is tempered by an interesting paradox at play in America. Yes, America tends to fall into Ahrimanic, materialistic worldviews and conditions, while at the same time

---

[57] Rudolf Steiner, "The Book of Revelation and the Work of the Priest," lecture of September 18, 1924.

[58] Rudolf Steiner, "The Mystery of the Double: Geographic Medicine," St. Gallen, lecture of November 16, 1917.

its younger forces, in relation to Europe, can preserve its future evolution. This paradox is highlighted by Steiner thus:

> We in Europe develop Anthroposophy out of the Spirit. Over there [in America] they develop something that is a kind of wooden doll of Anthroposophy. Everything becomes materialistic.
>
> But for one who is not a fanatic, there is something similar in American culture to what is anthroposophical science in Europe. Only everything there is wooden, it is not yet alive. We can make it alive in Europe out of the Spirit: those over there take it out of instinct. . . .
>
> It is in fact so interesting that in America materialism simply flourishes, but actually on the way to the Spirit; while in Europe if someone becomes a materialist he dies as human being. The American is a young materialist. In fact, all children are at first materialistic, and then grow to what is not materialism. So too will the American blatant materialism sprout to a spiritual element. That will be when the sun rises in the Sign of Aquarius.[59]

Lincoln's presidency had the effect of preserving America's youthfulness and leaving the doors open to the cosmopolitan impulses that streamed from spirit realms to earth at the beginning of Michael's regency.

---

[59] Rudolf Steiner, "Color and the Human Races," lecture of March 3, 1923.

Chapter 4

Lincoln and the Conduct of War

FROM EARLY ON LINCOLN'S STRATEGY for winning the war was tied to the blockade of Southern harbors, through strangling the trade with Great Britain upon which the South depended. It was a delicate enterprise, as it hinged upon carefully treading a delicate balance with international powers, chiefly Great Britain and France.

At the outbreak of the war it was clear that France and Great Britain saw their interests aligned with those of the Confederacy. France took advantage of it only a few months later by occupying Mexico and appointing Ferdinand Maximilian, an ally of the Confederacy, to the throne. The British Army consolidated its presence of 11,000 troops close to the Canada border, and its fleet was placed on wartime alert.

On the other hand the North could count on the sympathies of Tsar Alexander II, bent on contrasting the plans of his enemies, France and Great Britain. This possible alliance cautioned France and England from engaging in open war. At the time of the issuing of the Emancipation Proclamation, Tsar Alexander II did in effect station part of his Baltic fleet in Alexandria, Virginia, and part of his Pacific fleet in San Francisco, with orders to attack commercial shipping in case of war.

Another danger threatened the home front, in fact the capital. Maryland insurgents threatened Washington's communications and resupplies by cutting the telegraph lines and destroying the bridge linking Baltimore with the North. To protect the conduct of war from internal saboteurs or spies and still preserve the constitutional values to which he was undoubtedly committed, Lincoln had to take draconian legal measures. Such was the much-decried suspension of habeas corpus. At the time, however, it was only enforced along the route linking Washington, D.C., and Philadelphia. D. H. Donald estimates the number of people detained without trial to some 864 in the first nine months of the war, and larger numbers in the following years. However, most of those were in effect spies, blockade runners, foreign nationals, and smugglers. Political prisoners were a small minority.[60]

So much for internal enemies. Another matter was that of difficult alliances, even within one's own party. Adding some relief, Lincoln's archrival Stephen Douglas died in June 1861, leaving behind a demoralized Democratic Party, overwhelmed by large Republican majorities in both House and Senate. However, Lincoln had to navigate pleasing the constituencies of his party and balancing out interests of easterners and westerners, not to mention accommodating the border states in which slavery still persisted, lest they join the Confederacy. Within the party Lincoln had difficult relationships facing the pressure of radicals for whom the president's steps were too slow and his positions seemingly evasive.

Not least of all Lincoln found the need of involving himself on the theater of war, finding his generals often too timid or inept. Taking his role of commander in chief to heart, he took it upon himself to follow military operations up close, even studying Henry W. Halleck's *Elements of Military Art and Science.*

Dealing with Slavery

In the first two years in office Lincoln took small steps in curtailing the *Dred Scott* decision, by limiting the extension of slavery in the territories. In April 1862 he signed a new treaty with Great Britain for the suppression of the Atlantic slave trade. But, overall, this was a theme that he treaded lightly for fear of endangering precarious alliances, especially with the border states. The conduct of war raised enough delicate issues, such as the matter of runaway slaves reaching Union territory, which were unwanted in the Northern states.

At this point Lincoln explored the possibility of colonization—the relocation of the formerly enslaved in Africa or Latin America—and of

---

[60] David Herbert Donald, *Lincoln*, 304.

buying them from the slaveholders. He received support for the idea from a broad spectrum of factions and from public opinion. He reasoned that buying the slaves' freedom would be far less costly than the conduct of war; that an estimated eighty-seven days of war would cost the freedom of all the enslaved people in the border states and in the capital.[61] Although the idea met with some success in Washington, border states' representatives remained silent.

Beyond the Union's borders the issue of emancipation struck at a delicate balance of power and interests. Although Lincoln had signed Confiscation Acts, affecting the slaves of supposedly rebel slaveholders, those had been virtually ineffective.

The Emancipation Proclamation

The circumstances leading to the proclamation and Lincoln's resolution to announce it are well documented. Lincoln foresaw that formerly enslaved people would soon want to join the Union Army, but that would pose the thorny problem of acceptance from the enlisted men and hierarchy, and of integration. He also feared that as long as the war was not fought on the higher ground of a fight against slavery, France and England would be left free to throw their support to the Confederacy.

The decision to resort to an Emancipation Proclamation caused Lincoln much loss of sleep, first of all because of its shaky constitutional grounding. He could not measure its efficiency, and he wanted to resort to it when the Union Army would show itself in position of strength. It could not appear to be a desperate measure to turn the tide of events. Gideon Welles, Secretary of the Navy, reported to F. B. Carpenter that "[Lincoln] had made a vow, a covenant, that if God gave us victory in the approaching battle (which had just been fought) he would consider it his duty to move forward in the cause of emancipation." Secretary Chase reported much the same. After the success at the battle of Antietam, Lincoln considered the time was right.

The Emancipation Proclamation was envisioned as a temporary act of war, meant to be accompanied by other constitutional amendments, which included financial incentives to the states, compensated emancipation, and colonization.

---

[61] David Herbert Donald, *Lincoln*, 347.

As Lincoln had feared, the proclamation caused fracture lines among the Republicans, and tension in the border states. On the other hand it strengthened the peace element in the Democrats, and the Confederacy's resolve to fight. Most of all it had the desired effect abroad. In the summer and fall of 1862, both Great Britain and France had initiated steps to support the Confederacy, inspired by the latter's military victories. After the issuing of the proclamation, great crowds in London, Birmingham, and other cities cheered at the news, rendering all but impossible British to support for the Confederacy.

Lincoln pursued a long-term vision of change. Part of this was the establishment of loyal governments in Confederacy states, e.g., in Louisiana, which would send representatives to Washington. Ironically, these states would be exempted from the provisions of the Emancipation Proclamation. This meant being ready to accept a united nation but with slavery still in place.

After the issuing of the Emancipation Proclamation Union armies were defeated or brought to a standstill almost everywhere. Conservative and radical Republicans joined as critics of the president. Dissension plagued his own administration, and Lincoln struggled to hold it together and save the appearances. Seward resigned on December 16, and Lincoln kept his decision secret. He did the same with Chase's resignation and with that of Secretary of War Stanton. And there were rumblings in the army as well, particularly on the Potomac front.

Other threats loomed over Lincoln's wartime strategies. Buoyed by their successes in the 1862 fall elections, the Democrats wanted to negotiate peace with the South through the mediation of the French emperor. They rode on the wave of the many who had grown tired of the bloodshed and prolonged stalemate. The president had to take into account that abolitionism was a rare stance as most of public opinion was indifferent to the slavery issue; on the contrary, much of the American public feared a perceived possible invasion by ex-slaves (see Box: Racism in the North).

Racism in the North

Before the Civil War, Ohio, Indiana, Illinois, Iowa, and Oregon legally prohibited free Black people from settling within their borders or required them to post prohibitive bonds for "good behavior." In the remaining states, Black people were relegated to the most menial, low-paying jobs and consigned to segregated schools if they existed; most often they could not give testimony in courts nor ever serve on juries.

In many states in which they could previously vote—a right received after the Revolutionary War—Black people were now denied. This happened in New Jersey in 1807, in Connecticut in 1818, and in Pennsylvania in 1838. In 1821 New York Black voters had to fulfill property requirements, which had been set aside for white men. The only states that never denied Black men the right to vote were Maine, New Hampshire, Vermont, and Massachusetts.

In Northern politics Democrats played on the fears of their voters by convincing them that Republicans favored racial equality. Republicans tried to reassure their electorate by their commitment to white supremacy. No political movement could succeed across the North if they questioned the hierarchy of the races.

Catholic archbishop John Hughes, speaking on behalf of New York City's large Irish population, declared that Catholics "are willing to fight to the death for the support of the Constitution, the government, and the laws of the country. But if . . . they are to fight for the abolition of slavery, they will turn away in disgust from the discharge of what would otherwise be a patriotic duty." And in New York working-class fear of Black competition on the workplace led to the July 1863 four-day riots against the new federal Conscription Act. In those days a majority of angry Irish workers destroyed African-American homes, burned an African-American orphanage, and lynched a half-dozen African-Americans.

Between 1820 and 1850, free Black people were often targeted by mob violence, looting, and destroying or burning down Black homes, churches, schools, and public spaces. Black people were often stoned or beaten, and sometimes murdered.

One of the worst theaters of such violence was Philadelphia. Here African Americans were excluded from concert halls, schools, churches, public transportation, and other public spaces. They were also forced out of the skilled professions they had previously held.

When the Civil War ended, nineteen of twenty-four Union states still disfranchised Black voters. Only New England states with minuscule Black populations were an exception. Overall, only 6–7 percent of adult Black males could legally vote in the North at war's end.

Because many were even envisioning abandoning the Union to join the Confederacy, a further suspension of habeas corpus was used to suppress rebellion against administration policies. In the party Lincoln was attacked by the Republicans, particularly Thaddeus Stevens and the radical faction, which wanted to treat the South as a conquered nation.

The war had become unpopular. Due to the failure of new conscription, or of the incentives for returning soldiers, Lincoln realized he would need to enlist the freed slaves. In fact, the president gradually moved toward accelerating their enlistment. In opposition to the draft, in July 1863 big riots erupted in New York City, and others in Ohio, Pennsylvania, and Indiana. In New York City the riots were accompanied with looting and burning, and the deaths of more than one hundred.

Before the fall of 1863 the victories at Gettysburg and Vicksburg brought some relief to Lincoln and the Republican Party; however, they also strengthened desire for early peace. This carried the risk of abandoning all measures to deal with slavery and ceasing the recruitment of Black soldiers. The president refused to contemplate coming to terms with the Jefferson Davis administration. He launched his reelection bid with his "letter to Conkling" that was published in most major newspapers throughout the country. Lincoln used it to educate public opinion on the administration's political choices. Having been well received from public figures and the public at large, Lincoln added it to others he had written in relation to the draft, or those concerning other war-related issues. Published altogether as *The Letters of President Lincoln on Questions of National Policy*, they reached wide circulation.

Lincoln appointed General Grant to the head of the new division of the Mississippi, and this brought some immediate military successes. The victories came at a very politically opportune moment and boosted Lincoln's public support.

Gettysburg: Renewing Commitment to the Union

The timing of the Gettysburg and Vicksburg victories could not have been more propitious for Lincoln: July 4. He capitalized on these in order to press for favorable longer-term solutions. He saw that the growing national desire for peace carried the risk of dubious outcomes, and he wanted public opinion to acquire a better understanding of the issue at stake. The opportunity presented itself with the dedication of the Gettysburg [National] Cemetery where the fallen had been newly buried.

In the address he stressed the United States, not just as an Union, but as a nation—the word was used five times—whose origins he traced not to 1789, but to 1776. This placed equality at the center of the address, and spread the notion that the war had to continue until the promises of the Declaration of Independence were honored, that "all men are created equal" and until "government of the people, by the people, for the people, shall not perish from the earth."

The address became a success nationwide. Riding on its success, Lincoln extended the scope of the war, from preservation of the Union to include equality. Fate responded kindly with more decisive Union victories in November, and with the arrival of the czar's fleets at the Atlantic and Pacific harbors. This further dissuaded France and Britain from entering the fray.

The Continuation of War

The winter of 1863–64 caused fresh worries for the president: no progress on the military front and no new volunteers joining the army. New drafts called for 500,000 men on February 1 and 200,000 on March 14. Though Lincoln was burdened by the human cost of the war, he also wanted it to have served a purpose in the direction of the nation's destiny.

It must have been a huge relief to know that he could finally entrust overview of the military operations to Ulysses Grant, whom he appointed general-in-chief, title that had been bestowed only to George Washington and Winfield Scott before him. Grant, unlike other generals, wholeheartedly approved of Lincoln's Emancipation Proclamation and his enlistment of Black soldiers. He developed ambitious campaigns and attacked General Lee, even though success would still take time. Most of all he was resolute, and would not withdraw easily.

A June 1864 Baltimore Convention brought the main faction of the Republican Party together with some so-called War Democrats. It endorsed Lincoln's choices of a future constitutional amendment to abolish slavery and an unconditional surrender of the Confederacy. It chose as vice-president

Andrew Johnson, who as a Tennessee Union loyalist had endorsed Lincoln's Reconstruction program.

Before the reelection campaign, Lincoln had to tackle some serious threats to his constitutional views. The reconstructed state of Louisiana had reinstated the antebellum constitution, which offered no rights to Black people. For Lincoln, this was, if necessary, a reminder of the imperative of passing a constitutional amendment on the question of slavery and Black people's rights. Lincoln had to accommodate his principled stance on rights with his lenient and generous views about Reconstruction.

By mid-1864 continuing military defeats besieged Lincoln's future prospects; so did the difficulties of financing the war. The capital was newly in danger after Confederates were pressing upon Fort Stevens, just south of Richmond. Pressures increased for settling the war through negotiations and questionable compromises. The Republicans were divided, while the Democrats, rallying behind a peace platform, were likely to select McClellan, who would have sought an armistice, granting independence to the Confederacy. In the end the Democrats rallied in favor of the Union, but for an end to the fighting as well. Lincoln continued to push for an unconditional surrender and for abolition, arguing that support of Black regiments had been crucial in war operations, since there were some 200,000 of them enlisted at the time.

Finally, good news came from the war front, with General Sherman capturing Atlanta in early September, and Mobile surrendering soon after. This gave a great boost to Lincoln's chances for reelection. In the end although McClellan received 45% of the popular vote, the Republicans carried every state except Delaware, Kentucky, and New Jersey. The soldier vote went overwhelmingly to Lincoln.

Preserving America's Future

Winning a war often means losing national sovereignty. The danger of the Civil War was not only tangible in the physical presence of adversary armies ready to forge alliances with the Confederacy. War is a very costly enterprise, and assuring the financial support of operations can be very compromising in terms of the country's future. Very often this means losing economic sovereignty to the powers that finance the war. And Lincoln seems to have been aware of the dangers of financial dependence.

It is remarkable that the Lincoln's administration pursued the conduct of war without rationings, price controls, or recourse to a central bank. In economic and financial matters Lincoln trusted the opinions of Henry Carey, whose economic ideas were quite well-known at the time. Carey wanted to avoid a currency backed by gold, fearing that in times of instability a negative balance of trade is the engine driving a flow of gold outside of the country. Therefore he promoted a national currency, which would not flow out of the United States and could not be controlled by foreign influences.

To sustain the war effort, government spending was increased by 600% and cheap credit was offered to production efforts. Before the issuing of the later famous "greenbacks," the banknotes issued by state banks were backed by silver or gold. And eastern banks were ready to lend money to the government, but at a staggering 24% to 36% rates.[62]

The U.S. notes were printed on their back with green ink, hence their popular name. They were receipts that would acknowledge work done or goods offered, and they could likewise be traded for either one of these. They basically represented labor-hours.

In a first effort to finance the war in July 1861, Congress authorized $50,000,000 in demand notes, which bore no interest and could be redeemed for specie "on demand." They had no legal tender status yet. Until December 1861 they were fully redeemable in gold.

The greenbacks were rendered legal tender early in 1862; they did not need to be redeemed in precious metal and could be used for all private debts, though not for taxes and duties. Remarkably, even through the inflationary process of an extended war, by December 1865 a greenback was still redeemable at 68 cents per gold dollar! It has been calculated that the U.S. was spared the fate of a crippling $4 billion interest debt.[63] Lincoln's well-advised policies spared the Union from the fate of so many other ex-colonies, and close to home that of Simon Bolivar's Gran Colombia.

Even after the National Banking Act of 1863, which allowed nationally chartered banks to issue and lend currency, due to popular pressure an

---

[62] Ellen Hodgson Brown, *The Web of Debt*, 83.
[63] Ellen Hodgson Brown, *The Web of Debt*, 87.

outstanding $346 million worth of greenbacks remained in circulation as part of the nation's currency, tempering the rise of the national debt.[64]

Lincoln's Leadership

Lincoln was an extremely social individual—social in the sense of being interested in and able to understand people. He spent much of his time in social intercourse. As a president he not only met with soldiers in the frontlines; he also visited hospitals, attended funerals, and sat in during regular working sessions of Congress. He constantly sought firsthand information. He could break with etiquette and enter other members' cabinets to witness the proceedings, and he actively sought to meet with his cabinet members in between official meetings. He was probably the most accessible president the nation has ever had. Add to this that he was most often pleasant, encouraging, and humorous.

The president was eager to recognize the sharpest minds and the most dependable collaborators. He chose his people according to their objective skills, rather than their loyalty to him. And he worked closely with them, eager to improve their relationship. For every failed relationship, like those of McClellan or Salmon Chase, there were two or more successes.

Even with those with whom he parted ways, the president was rarely vindictive. He could show a high degree of flexibility with insubordination, but not with indifference and passivity, however. Salmon Chase, who had offered his resignations four times, is a good case in point. Lincoln finally accepted his pro forma resignation, much to his surprise. Later, however, he nominated Sen. William P. Fessenden, one of Chase's strongest supporters, to be the new secretary of the treasury. And he soon appointed Chase to be the new chief justice of the Supreme Court. He was the one administering the oath of office to Lincoln on the occasion of the second inaugural.

Throughout his days in office, Lincoln offered his subordinates encouragement, support, and ways to get to know each other. However, he did not lack a clear sense of boundaries, and gave clear messages of how far they could or could not go. He had little care for preserving harmony if it

---

[64] Ellen Hodgson Brown, *The Web of Debt*, 94.

meant sacrificing principles. He was very clear once an infraction touched something he deeply cared about. He did this while preserving dignity and, possibly, deepening mutual respect. Examples of this survive in the detailed letters he wrote to his subordinates, in which he could be very diplomatic but also candid. To General Joseph Hooker, after complimenting him, he wrote: "And yet I think it best for you to know that there are some things in regard to which, I am not quite satisfied with you." And he added exactly what he expected of him. The general recalled being deeply impressed by the honesty and told a newspaperman it was "just such a letter as a father might write to his son."[65] On the other hand he never quarreled over insignificant matters and would know how to avoid conflict when not absolutely necessary. Overall he had a penetrating understanding of human nature, allied to an ability to forgive.

Lincoln was a master in garnering persuasion; he knew the art of creative compromise, which would meet most parties' needs. He had already shown it at age twenty-seven, when he was able to mastermind the transfer of the Illinois state capital from Vandalia to Springfield, through clever bargaining. His already quoted speech at the Temperance Society shows what persuasion meant to him: "When the conduct of men is designed to be influenced, *persuasion,* kind, unassuming persuasion, should ever be adopted." Following these mental habits, it was very normal for the president to consult frequently with members of his cabinet and avoid doing anything concerning a department without consulting with its heads. He knew the value of making requests versus giving orders, and using suggestions and recommendations. And most of those who collaborated with Lincoln had the feeling of being special to him.

The president also showed great resilience under stress and criticism. He would most often ignore attacks, especially when they expressed petty concerns. He wrote on April 11, 1865, "As a general rule, I abstain from reading the reports of attacks upon myself, wishing not to be provoked by that to which I can not properly offer an answer."[66] He could view unjust criticism with amusement, rather than anger. To Stephen Douglas's accusations in 1858 he replied, "When a man hears himself somewhat misrepresented, it provokes him—at least, I find it so with myself; but

---

[65] Donald T. Phillips, *Lincoln on Leadership: Executive Strategies for Tough Times,* 45–46.

[66] Public address of April 11, 1865, quoted in Donald T. Phillips, *Lincoln on Leadership,* 69.

when the misrepresentation becomes very gross and palpable, it is more apt to amuse him." However, he reacted if the attacks could impact public perception of his views and principles, as he expressed in a speech in 1859: "I have found that it is not entirely safe, when one is misrepresented under his very nose, to allow the misrepresentation to go uncontradicted." He spent a lot of time and consideration on how to react most appropriately. To master his emotions and understand a complex situation, Lincoln used to draft letters to the people with whom he was upset, which he often would not send. He could thus better understand the situation, and in the end weigh the pros and cons of sending them. In the process of writing, he could reach greater clarity.

Lincoln had no doubt understood in his youth the importance of balancing passion with reason. He had acquired a great degree of mastery over his emotions. He most often recognized credit where it was due and was ready to assume responsibility when things went wrong. This supported his subordinates and encouraged them to take risks and innovate.

Lincoln was a bundle of apparent polarities and contradictions; he was a master of paradox. He was greatly flexible while also a model of consistency. The president did in fact show his flexible approach quite candidly: "My policy is to have no policy; I shall not surrender this game leaving any available card unplayed." And, in pure Mercurial fashion he was always open for a change of mind: "I shall do less whenever I shall believe what I am doing hurts the cause, and I shall do more whenever I shall believe doing more will help the cause. I shall try to correct errors when shown to be errors; and I shall adopt new views so fast as they shall appear to be true views."[67]

Most of all the president showed great resilience and perseverance. Lincoln rarely, if ever, gave up after failures. After losing to Stephen Douglas he wrote: "The fight must go on. The cause of civil liberty must not be surrendered at the end of one or even hundred defeats."[68] And in order to achieve very ambitious goals, Lincoln knew how to set up realistic, attainable small steps. Thus during the war he concentrated on the destruction of Lee's army rather than the capture of the Confederate capital.

In the long search for the ideal general, Lincoln took on the work with

---

[67] Letter to Horace Greeley of August 22, 1862.
[68] Letter to Henry Asbury of November 19, 1858.

the army very methodically. His first step was to completely reorganize and redirect the armed forces from 16,000 men to over half a million at the end of the war. Lincoln went through quite a few generals before arriving at Ulysses Grant. However, even when they were inept, he learned everything he could in terms of strategy from them. When he needed to build, organize, and train the army, he selected George McClellan, who was perfect for this job, but would not fight. When McClellan failed him, Lincoln moved him to command just the Army of the Potomac. Seeing the need for urgency, he did not hesitate to step in when his subordinate tarried. Thus he personally directed the assault on Norfolk before its capture.

Lincoln had great care in preventing operations from coming to a standstill, while preserving the dignity of individuals. When a general was not performing, he would remove some responsibility and authority from him. If the pattern continued, he would remove the individual out of the decision-making, by having him report to another superior. In this way Lincoln had to accept disappointment from quite a few generals. When he finally found the man he could trust in Ulysses Grant, he gave him full responsibility. Even after he delegated most authority to Grant, Lincoln never ceased to follow closely military operations and exert his personal influence when he felt it necessary. The selection and testing of his generals was in fact an enduring task for the president (See box).

Similar patterns often happened on the political front, where the president had to deal with a cabinet rendered famous as a "team of rivals." Lincoln showed he was able to determine what was really going on, and he often found creative ways in which to confront and defuse tensions. The president was in the habit of bringing all dissenting parties to the table and pushing them to find a way to make peace. An example: in 1862 Chase led the charge to discredit Seward, whom he wanted to replace. The seasoned senator was being unjustly accused on many accounts by various Republican senators inspired by Chase. Lincoln invited all parties except Seward to a special session of the cabinet, asking them to iron out all differences before they left. The senators did not know the cabinet would be present and vice-versa, placing Chase in the awkward position of not being able to support what the senators would say, without clearly showing his role in leading the dissent.

Lincoln and His Generals

President Lincoln took to heart his role of commander-in-chief; all the more so because the army lacked for a long spell a true general-in-chief. During that time Lincoln took on the role. The following is the sequence of choices directly taken by Lincoln himself.

1861: The army was under the command of 75-year-old General Winfield Scott. Lincoln personally oversaw the reorganization of the Armed Forces. He agreed with the general on the importance of securing the Mississippi River and of blockading the Southern harbors.

March 1861: He appointed Irvin C. McDowell as commanding general and relieved Scott of most of his duties, while still consulting with him.

July 1861: Realizing the need for an organizer able to rebuild and train the army, he appointed General George B. McClellan, first to the Army of the Potomac, then as general-in-chief.

March 1862: He relieved McClellan of his command and confined him to the Army of the Potomac, appointing General Henry W. Walleck as head of the Department of the Mississippi and General John C. Fremont of the Mountain Department. During this time he took initiative from the hands of General McClellan to personally orchestrate the attack and capture of Norfolk, Virginia.

July 1862: Walleck is named general-in-chief, McClellan having to report to him. Walleck did not show capacity and initiative. Lincoln appointed John A. McClernand to the Department of the Mississippi, William S. Rosecrans to the Mountain Department, and General Nathaniel P. Banks to the newly formed Department of the Gulf. All generals reported to Lincoln and took orders from him.

November 1862: He appointed Ambrose E. Burnside as commander of the Army of the Potomac. Burnside was relieved of his task only two months later and replaced by General Joe Hooker, who would himself be replaced by General George G. Meade by June 1863.

February 1863: General Ulysses S. Grant takes charge of the Department of the Mississippi.

October 1863: Grant takes command of the armies of the West.

March 1864: Lincoln promotes Grant to lieutenant general, giving him command of all the armies.

He was thus forced to agree that Seward had acted properly and honestly. With such a strategy Lincoln embarrassed both senators and Chase, exposing the latter as an impostor who could not be trusted. Seward was cleared of all charges, and the next day Lincoln accepted Chase's resignation.

Lincoln and the Fruits of Previous Incarnations

"When a first-class mind is filtered through an inferior one, it becomes unrecognizable. That is why there are so many different Lincolns. We see him through lesser minds," Susan B. Martinez asserts.[69] Recapturing Lincoln's essential being has in fact been the effort of seeing him through many great minds of our nation before attempting a synthesis.

The way in which Lincoln integrated paradoxes and polarities is a sign of a likely previous life initiation, as seems the case with Franklin and Washington. Many historians can but marvel at how the president embodied one quality and its seeming opposite.

Donald T. Phillips, as one of many, finds the sixteenth president "charismatic, yet unassuming; consistent yet flexible; victim of vast amounts of slander, yet very popular with the troops; trusting and compassionate and demanding and tough; risk-taker yet patient and calculating."[70] This compounding of seeming opposites is in fact the essence of initiation when it reemerges instinctively in the will; it renders the individual able to naturally synthesize polarities. In terms of planetary qualities we could point out how Lincoln embodied each polarity:

- He conducted the Civil War fully, almost relentlessly, out of a Mars gesture. He spoke his mind diplomatically but candidly, and he did not broach insubordination. He knew when to seize an opportunity. On the other hand he discharged his fatherly duties and attended to his friendships in a complete Venus fashion. He was imbued with deep interest in fellow human beings, regardless of their station in life.

[69] Susan B. Martinez, *The Psychic Life of Abraham Lincoln*, 133.
[70] Donald T. Phillips, *Lincoln on Leadership: Executive Strategies for Tough Times*, 79.

- He could coat everything he approached with Mercurial wit. He knew how to avoid conflict. He also acted out of Jupiterian wisdom: he knew what was possible and what wasn't, and recognized when it was necessary to wait.
- He had the Saturnian long view that saw centuries ahead. He could see before most of his fellow citizens the implications of political or judicial decisions. However, he respected tradition and precedent within the Moon spirit; he took no liberties with the Constitution. He subordinated his far sight to the necessary limitations of time and space. He balanced desire for change with patient education.
- His generosity of spirit attests to his continuous Sun-like qualities; so do his views about Christ and His deed for the redemption of humanity, and his unwavering trust in the hand of Providence. He knew how to mediate and act with magnanimity. He forgave naturally and rarely, if ever, took revenge.

Through his leadership Lincoln preserved America's cosmopolitan essence. He preserved its spirit and made it possible for America to enter in the right way into the cosmopolitan Michaelic age, characterized by Steiner thus:

> You see, the cosmopolitan views . . . are simply a reflection of what occurred in the spiritual world. The tendency exists in mankind to wipe out the various differences which were fostered by the blood and the nerve temperament. It is not a tendency of the spiritual worlds to create further differences among mankind, but it is a tendency of the spiritual worlds to pour a cosmopolitan element over mankind.[71]

Or to echo Emerson's final words of his "American Scholar" address: "A nation of men will for the first time exist, because each believes himself inspired by the Divine Soul which also inspires all men." He implied that America can grasp everything anew and make it her own through her own forces.

---

[71] Rudolf Steiner, Munich, lecture of February 17, 1918.

Fruits of Previous Initiations

"When a first-class mind is filtered through an inferior one, it becomes unrecognizable. That is why there are so many different Lincolns. We see him through lesser minds" quotes Susan B. Martinez.[72] Recapturing Lincoln's essential being has in fact been the effort of seeing him through many great minds of our nation before attempting a synthesis.

The way in which Lincoln integrated paradoxes and polarities is a sign of a likely previous life initiation, as seems the case with Franklin and Washington. Many historians can but marvel at how the president embodied one quality and its seeming opposite.

Donald T. Phillips, as one of many, finds the sixteenth president "charismatic, yet unassuming; consistent yet flexible; victim of vast amounts of slander, yet very popular with the troops; trusting and compassionate and demanding and tough; risk-taker yet patient and calculating."[73] This compounding of seeming opposites is in fact the essence of initiation when it reemerges instinctively in the will; it renders the individual able to naturally synthesize polarities. In terms of planetary qualities we could point out how Lincoln embodied each polarity:

- He conducted the Civil War fully, almost relentlessly, out of a Mars gesture. He spoke his mind diplomatically but candidly and did not broach insubordination. He knew when to seize an opportunity. On the other hand he discharged his fatherly duties and attended to his friendships in a complete Venus fashion. He was imbued with deep interest in fellow human beings, regardless of their station in life.

- He could coat everything he approached with Mercurial wit. He knew how to avoid conflict. He acted out of Jupiterian wisdom; he knew what was possible and what wasn't, and recognized when it was necessary to wait.

- He had the Saturnian long view that saw centuries ahead. He could see before most of his fellow citizens the implications of political or judicial decisions. However, he respected tradition and precedent within the Moon spirit; he took no liberties with

---

[72] Susan B. Martinez, *The Psychic Life of Abraham Lincoln*, 133.

[73] Donald T. Phillips, *Lincoln on Leadership: Executive Strategies for Tough Times*, 79.

the Constitution. He subordinated his far sight to the necessary limitations of time and space. He balanced desire for change with patient education.

- His generosity of spirit attest to his continuous Sun-like qualities; so do his views about Christ and His deed for the redemption of humanity, and his unwavering trust in the hand of Providence. He knew how to mediate and act with magnanimity. He forgave naturally and rarely, if ever, took revenge.

Through his leadership Lincoln preserved America's cosmopolitan essence. It preserved its spirit and made it possible for America to enter in the right way into the cosmopolitan Michaelic age, characterized by Steiner thus:

> You see, the cosmopolitan views . . . are simply a reflection of what occurred in the spiritual world. The tendency exists in mankind to wipe out the various differences which were fostered by the blood and the nerve temperament. It is not a tendency of the spiritual worlds to create further differences among mankind, but it is a tendency of the spiritual worlds to pour a cosmopolitan element over mankind.[74]

Or, to echo Emerson's final words of his American Scholar address: "A nation of men will for the first time exist, because each believes himself inspired by the Divine Soul which also inspires all men." He implied that America can grasp everything anew and make it her own through her own forces.

---

[74] Rudolf Steiner, Munich, lecture of February 17, 1918.

Chapter 5

Educating the Nation

A PRESIDENT OF LINCOLN'S STATURE and a national emergency such as a Civil War are likely to have left a deep imprint on American government and its conduit. Certainly the power of the executive came out strengthened from Lincoln's tenure; yet the American Constitution survived with grace one of its greatest challenges. How was this made possible?

We are left to wonder that it was during one of America's greatest trials that the ideal of the Declaration of Independence was renewed and strengthened; the signing of the Thirteenth Amendment was no small achievement for a nation still at war, even if close to its ending. All of these outcomes stem in great measure from the president's grasp of the nation's founding documents and the spirit that animated them. We could say that Lincoln reconnected the nation to its deepest impulses, or at least offered an impetus and an opportunity in that direction, though we know that much was left undone through Reconstruction—but that is something we cannot impute to the president.

Behind all of such unlikely achievements at the nation's eleventh hour stand not only Lincoln's views on legal matters and his strategic choices. More than ever stands a unique personality. We will look at layer after layer of Lincoln's soul and spirit to reach the core of his convictions and outline the uniqueness of his spiritual life and being. Who was this individual who arrived at the right place and the right time to redress the course of history and preserve the United States' future?

The Declaration of Independence and the Constitution

In his July 4, 1861, address to the nation, Lincoln stated the kernel of the problem he faced throughout his presidency: "Must a government of necessity be too strong for the liberties of its people or too weak to maintain its own existence." There could be no better characterization of the nation's challenge at the time in which Lincoln took the reins of power. The South wanted to part ways, and many Radicals and Democrats were strong advocates of disunion because of the issue of slavery. More than one force pushed toward the nation's dismemberment.

Partly because of the exceptional circumstances of his presidency, Lincoln redefined the American presidency and revised the American constitutional system. In a letter to Albert Hodges of April 4, 1864, he explained the conundrum under which a constitutionalist like him had to operate:

> My oath . . . imposed upon me the duty of preserving, by every indispensable means, that government—that nation—of which that Constitution was the organic law. Was it possible to lose the nation, and yet preserve the Constitution? By general law life and limb must be protected; yet often a limb must be amputated to save a life; but a life is never wisely given to save a limb. I felt that measures, otherwise unconstitutional, might become lawful, by becoming indispensable to the preservation of the Constitution, through the preservation of the nation.

In his earliest speeches Lincoln was already calling for support to the rule of law and the Constitution, which he probably studied first in the early 1830s. His work as a lawyer, although not directly concerned with the Constitution, had already given him a pragmatic approach toward complex issues.

Between the broad constructionism of Alexander Hamilton and the strict constructionism of Thomas Jefferson, Lincoln inclined more to the latter, but only to a certain point. Where he departed from strict constructionism in particular was in the role of the government in supporting economic development. He was overall loath to taking liberties with the Constitution and stretching it for partisan interests. Americans at the time had a view of government such that it should not intervene in local matters. The views of abolitionists were seen as radical for this reason.

In constitutional matters Brian R. Dirck sees the Declaration of Independence as an added focus of Lincoln since 1852.[75] In Henry Clay's eulogy Lincoln pointed to those who were attacking the Declaration and its tenet of equality. He wanted to show that the Constitution itself was antislavery by placing the Declaration of Independence at the heart of our institutions, the Constitution as their blueprint. He wrote: "Without the Constitution and the Union, we could not have attained [national prosperity] . . . but even these are not the cause of our great prosperity. There is something back of these, entwining itself more closely about the human heart. That something, is the principle that clears the path for all—gives hope to all—and by consequence . . . the expression of that principle, in our Declaration of Independence, was most happy and fortunate." And further: "The Union and the Constitution are the picture of silver, subsequently framed around it. . . . The picture was made, not to conceal, or destroy the apple; but to adorn and preserve it. The picture was made for the apple—not the apple for the picture." This is a metaphor taken from Proverbs 25:11.

The Struggle for the Declaration of Independence

In returning to politics, Lincoln's first adversary was Roger B. Taney, chief justice of the Supreme Court, who wanted to introduce proslavery interpretations throughout the Constitution. Taney turned the *Dred Scott* decision into a battle-horse for the South. He wanted to exclude African-Americans from every notion of rights and citizenship, emphasizing that they were held as inferior race at the time of the writing of the Constitution. For him this would have extended even to emancipated Black people. He explicitly stated that the negro was not included in the Declaration of Independence preamble. Moreover Taney emphasized the rights of property, wanting to treat African-Americans completely from this perspective. he enthused slaveholders of the South who were feeling they were been given future guarantees against any inroads on the slavery matter.

---

[75] Brian R. Dirck, *Lincoln and the Constitution*, 27–28.

For Lincoln the Declaration of Independence proclaimed an ideal toward which America could aspire, a possibility of evolution and improvement. The lines were drawn when Stephen Douglas explicitly endorsed the *Dred Scott* decision of the Court, even though it stood at odds with popular sovereignty, since it stated that no government legislation could limit slavery. Lincoln could not speak for racial equality that few Northerners were ready to accept. Nevertheless he had the courage to state "there is no reason in the world why the negro is not entitled to all the natural rights enumerated in the Declaration of Independence, the right to life, liberty and the pursuit of happiness." He perceived of his adversaries, "If they would repress all tendencies to liberty and ultimate emancipation . . . they must penetrate the human soul and eradicate the love of liberty."[76] And civil liberties were another thorny issue.

Suspension of Habeas Corpus

In a civil war it is very difficult to identify the enemies. If Maryland left the Union, the nation's survival would have been truly threatened. And the state was undoubtedly courting with secession.

For the suspension of the writ of habeas corpus, Lincoln could avail himself of his constitutional powers under Article I, Section 9. His litmus test came from Maryland, in a scenario that called for prompt action. The president authorized General Scott to suspend habeas corpus under a clearly defined criteria: military saboteurs. The endorsement was made easier by Scott being a Virginian. Lincoln then extended the reach and scope of arrests, but always within military lines. In May of that year this led to the arrest of John Merryman, accused of pro-Confederate activities; these were clearly proven since Merryman had been very outspoken.

Merryman filed a writ of habeas corpus with Taney, who granted the request. General Cadwalader, responsible for the arrest, did not back down. Taney argued for a very clear and confined awarding of presidential powers, even in wartime. He painted a dark picture of the dangers of Lincoln assuming more and more power and civil liberties being curtailed. He wanted to draw his adversary into a confrontation. Lincoln proved that he was acting well within his prerogatives and detailed his decision from a

---

[76] Lincoln-Douglas debate of August 21, 1858, Ottawa, IL.

legal-constitutional ground, refusing to attack Taney personally. He knew as a lawyer how to avoid open confrontation. He showed primarily the need to suspend habeas corpus as the only way to preserve all other constitutional guarantees. On the other hand he mustered support for his decision from various sides.

With Congress backing him, Lincoln diluted the effect of Taney's *Ex Parte Merryman*. Scholars researching the matter have concluded that Lincoln's use of the suspension of habeas corpus was on the whole rather moderate and that few abuses resulted from it. Even John Merryman was promptly released in July 1861.

Lincoln and the "Rebels"

Never before the Civil War did America's presidency so clearly require a lawyer, someone who would be able to preserve the Union but also the Constitution. The nation required someone with the will to take extraordinary measures, and yet not hunger for power.

Only someone like Lincoln could frame the issue of the Civil War within acceptable parameters, by setting the stage in such a way that the Confederates appeared as the aggressors and the government merely reacting to protect itself. This served the Union well in matters of international law and the international threat.

In rebutting the right to secede, Lincoln argued persuasively: "The Union is older than any of the States, and, in fact, it created them as States.... Not one of them ever had a State constitution independent of the Union."[77] And he could claim that there had been other secession attempts that had been put down before the Civil War.

Lincoln held that the Confederacy was not a legal entity, but that put him into a bind in more than one place. Normally the rebels should have been tried for treason, which under Article III, Section 3 places a high bar of proof. The article protected civil liberties, and treason trials had been extremely rare. Moreover such trials risked being overturned by the Supreme Court. In the end Confederate prisoners were treated like captives of a foreign nation, exchanging them or placing them in prisoner-of-war camps. To all practical purposes prisoners were treated as traitors and nontraitors, citizens

---

[77] Lincoln's July 4, 1861, Message to Congress.

and noncitizens, alien and nonalien enemy combatants. The Supreme court, in the *Prize* cases, allowed the president to have it both ways, because "He [the president] must determine what degree of force the crisis demands."[78]

During four years Lincoln carefully characterized the Civil War as "insurrection" and some other time as "rebellion." He never referred to the Confederate States of America, at most to the "so-called Confederate States of America." However, this stance was contradicted by the naval blockade imposed on Southern ports. Because he saw the war as the putting down of a rebellion, he felt justified in having neither negotiations nor a peace treaty at any time. And he saw the continuation of the war as something to be led primarily by the Executive, and its chief.

Another irony of the way of framing the question of rebellion versus secession was the delicate issue of West Virginia; here was the nation accepting in reverse terms that the rebels of a rebel state had the right . . . to secede. Lincoln was well aware of the constitutional conundrum, witness the slow pace of his decisions and his legal hesitations.

Lincoln and the Radicals

The Radicals represented a narrow cross-section of the American population; Lincoln could not align himself with them, especially from a strategic standpoint. He first tried to stay away from the slavery issue, though it immediately came to haunt him through the problem of runaway slaves coming to the North. Strictly speaking they were meant to be given back; but it was known that they contributed to the war effort. One of his generals and ex-politician, Benjamin Butler, came up with the idea of seizing them as prize of war, and they became known as "contraband." For this goal Congress passed the Property Confiscation Act in August 1861 that Lincoln signed into law. The law put an end to the property rights of rebel slaveholder but did not offer freedom to the slaves.

The Second Confiscation Act of 1862 awarded the slaves' freedom, while still allowing rebels to claim their "property" by joining the Union within a prescribed 60 days. In response to the drafting of the act, Lincoln voiced his objections on constitutional grounds in order to push Congress to

---

[78] Brian R. Dirck, *Lincoln and the Constitution*, 117–18.

amend it, specifying that "no property would be seized beyond the lifetime of any given Confederate property owner."

On the other hand, when generals close to the Radicals—e.g., General John C. Fremont—confiscated rebel property, and among this their slaves, emitting a proclamation of his own, Lincoln cracked down on him. He ordered Fremont to rescind his proclamation because he saw in it a violation of the Constitution in "punishing treason beyond the life of the traitor."

Lincoln was uniquely able to withstand two threats to the nation; the Confederacy who wanted to disintegrate the nation, and the Radicals who had too flexible a view of the Constitution and of how to expand its interpretation to suit their ideals. With them Lincoln may have secretly agreed with the ends, but little with the means.

Lincoln the Writer and Educator

According to the experience of all, Lincoln the orator was a spectacle to behold, one with endless variations and hues. D. H. Donald reports from various newspapers of 1848 that Lincoln could start a talk leaning against a wall, speaking as if it all were of little concern in indifferent tone. While he did this he gained control of his stance, "loosening his tongue, and firing up his thoughts, until he had got entire possession of himself and of his audience." These changes were reflected in his voice initially "sharp, shrill piping and squeaky" and later turning "harmonious, melodious and musical."[79] His voice projected to the farthest reaches of a large crowd gathered outdoors. And he often accompanied vocal expression with considerable body language.

Lincoln had a great sense of timing and could sense the mood of the crowd. He had a great memory for facts and figures, anecdotes, and humorous stories. He could charm his audience with a mercurial succession of arguments and anecdotes, common wisdom, and juicy tidbits. Lincoln combined a great deal of spontaneity, especially through his humor, with an almost obsessively methodical care for detail and preparation.

---

[79] David Herbert Donald, *Lincoln*, 132.

Humor and Spontaneity

Lincoln's humor evolved over the years. In his youth Lincoln told jokes and stories for their own sake. As a lawyer he found that wit, poking fun, and placing things in perspective supported his trade. As a politician he had been tempted at times by satire, and learned at personal cost to temper his passions. As a president humor served many purposes: proving a point and saving time, deflecting criticism, saying no without alienating, softening a rebuke, putting people at ease, avoiding an embarrassing commitment, and last but not least, not taking the situation or himself too seriously, witness his often self-deprecating comments or stories (see box on the next page).

Lincoln knew he was a good story-teller but did it always with a purpose in mind. "I believe I have the popular reputation of being a storyteller, but I do not deserve the name in its general sense, for it is not the story itself, but its purpose or effect that interests me. I often avoid a long and useless discussion by others, or a laborious explanation on my own part, by a short explanation on my own part, by a short story that illustrates my point of view."[80]

To General McClellan, who was not engaging the enemy, rather than venting his exasperation the president asked if he could borrow the army. To his cabinet, after the failure of the battle of Antietam, he decided to read a humorous story from Artemus Ward, laughing out loud about it. No one joined him, so the president asked "Gentlemen, why don't you laugh? With the fearful strain that is upon me night and day, if I did not laugh I should die, and you need this medicine as much as I do."[81] This is also what he stated to Herndon: "If it were not for the stories/jokes/jests I should die; they give vent—are the vents—of my moods and gloom."[82] It was in effect the finest medicine for moods of depression that could assail him.

---

[80] Donald T. Phillips, *Lincoln on Leadership: Executive Strategies for Tough Times*, 159.
[81] War Cabinet session of September 22, 1862.
[82] Susan B. Martinez, *The Psychic Life of Abraham Lincoln*, 97.

Lincoln about Himself and Stephen Douglas

Upon losing the 1859 election to Stephen Douglas and asked by a gentleman how he felt: "Well I feel just like the boy who stubbed his toe—too d——d badly hurt to laugh, and too d——d proud to cry!" (Paul Zall, 22)

One of many self-disparaging stories about his appearance attributed to Lincoln at the time of the Lincoln Douglas debates is that of the ugly man shouting to Lincoln "By George, I must shoot you; I made a vow that I would kill any man uglier than myself." And the reply "Fire away, stranger; if I'm uglier than you I don't want to live." (Paul Zall, 23)

Upon being nominated for a second term on June 7, 1864, and being told the only way he could be defeated would be for Grant to conquer Richmond and run for the presidency against him: "I feel very much like the man who said he didn't want to die particularly, but if he had got to die that would be precisely the disease he would like to die of." (Keith W. Jennison, 128)

"If I have one vice . . . it is not being able to say no! Thank God for not making me a woman. . . . But if He had I suppose he would have made me just as ugly as He did, and no one would have tempted me." (Paul Zall, xv)

Talking about Stephen Douglas in July 1847: "[The party politicians] have seen in his round, jolly, fruitful face, post offices, land offices, marshalships, and cabinet appointments, chargeships and foreign missions, bursting and sprouting out in wonderful exuberance." (Keith W. Jennison, 50)

About Douglas's reasoning, he commented that it was as "thin as the homeopathic soup that was made by boiling the shadow of a pigeon that had been starved to death." (Keith W. Jennison, 54)

And about Judge Douglas accusing him of selling liquor during the debates: "He forgot to tell you that, while I was on one side of the counter, the Judge was always on the other." (Keith W. Jennison, 57)

It was obvious that Douglas feared his adversary's humor: "Every one of his stories seems like a whack upon my back. . . . Nothing else—not any of his arguments or any of his replies to my questions—disturbs me. But when he begins to tell a story, I feel that I am to be overmatched." (Paul Zall, xvii)

With the lightness of his humor, Lincoln could convince almost everybody he talked to. He could also get rid of unsolicited requests without the originators being able to figure out how he had done it. With the ability to pull the right story for the right moment at will, he knew that common folk were more easily influenced through these than through logical arguments.

For all his lightness the politician, like the lawyer before him, was also deeply earnest and thorough in his preparations.

Planning and Method

Lincoln would often prepare his subject for days and weeks, and write down his speeches to the last word, depending on the impact he was seeking. He would even prepare for conversations he was going to have. As an example, at the conclusion of a meeting with General Hooker, he handed him a letter for him to further think about.[83]

Following his youthful urge to understand precise meanings, the older Lincoln knew the value of every single word he used. In response to those in his party who wanted to reprint his Cooper Union Address slightly modified here and there, Lincoln responded in the negative to even the most minor change suggestions. He was adamant: "I do not wish the sense changed, or modified, to a hair's breadth."[84] Likewise in his Fourth of July address to the nation, he did not want to use "secession" but rather "rebellion," not to concede a point to the Confederacy, and he went at length to explain the whys. Rebellion marked a distinct, violent act; secession would have conceded a legal choice, and legitimized it.

The same to the above is true in the negative. His most famous speeches or printed addresses excel in the choice of what to say and not to say, and how to say it in order to appeal to certain constituencies while not alienating the more fragile support of other ones, e.g., conciliate the Radicals without alienating the Border States.

Tactical Choices

Lincoln was used to reading the opposite side of every question even more thoroughly than the support arguments. In preparing for his debates with

---

[83] Donald T. Phillips, *Lincoln on Leadership: Executive Strategies for Tough Times*, 151.
[84] Douglas L. Wilson, *Lincoln's Sword: The Presidency and the Power of Words*, 43.

Douglas, he explained: "I sift Stephen Douglas's argument down to the subjects he evades or handles recklessly. I jot down those points and store them in my hat."[85]

In tackling the thorny issue of suspension of habeas corpus, Lincoln wanted to show that the rebels used the constitutional guarantees and freedoms to undermine the very same Constitution. He also chose an appropriate central image: the issue of the treatment of the deserters, who could lose their lives, while those who incited them sought protection by habeas corpus.

Lincoln was also a master of waiting to express his ideas by taking advantage of external, fortuitous circumstances and/or challenges thrown at him. Often, what he let out as an apparent spontaneous response to the challenge of the moment had in reality long been prepared, as we will see below in relation to the future announcement of the Emancipation Proclamation.

The president had learned that a man in his position, and in such exceptional circumstances could ill afford off-the-cuff comments or impromptu speeches. He had been targeted when early in his career he had spoken words to the effect that all men had been created equal in Chicago in 1858.

Let us look more closely at how Lincoln generated ideas and speeches. At first whatever thoughts crossed his mind were written on scraps of paper. He would do so, for example, while he was reading something. He would place the paper on his desk, or in his vest or pants pockets. If he was in a public space, he would ask for paper and pen when he would have time and inspiration to take down notes. When the time approached to deliver the speech, he would assemble all the scraps, revise them, and compose the letter or the speech. John G. Nicolai called it "process of cumulative thought" that would continue later with periodic revisions of the material gathered. Lincoln commented thus about his own process: "In that way I saved my best thoughts on the subject, and you know, such things often come in a kind of intuitive way more clearly than if one were to sit down and deliberately reason them out."[86] This denotes a very proactive attitude toward everything

---

[85] Susan B. Martinez, *The Psychic Life of Abraham Lincoln*, 228.

[86] Douglas L. Wilson, *Lincoln's Sword: The Presidency and the Power of Words*, 166.

that he was preparing to meet. He was actively anticipating the future and preparing for all sorts of possible scenarios and responses.

The process could include another variety of steps. Lincoln would gather input from trusted advisors or cabinet members, and look for speeches on similar themes that could provide inspiration. Finally, testing the speech for its intended effect was as important as the preliminary steps. He would often ask an individual to play the part of an audience. Most often he wasn't reading to elicit feedback; he just wanted to be able to judge the message by hearing it delivered, rather than read. "Nothing sounds the same when there isn't anybody to hear it and find fault with it."[87] He felt he could hardly judge what he wrote without hearing it. This was something Lincoln carried from his upbringing and original love for the spoken word.

Composition Techniques and Testing

Lincoln's self-made education showed in the overabundant and capricious use of commas, misspellings, haphazard capitalization. Part of this reflected the reality that the president composed from inner hearing, and for the effect on his listeners. It was noticeable in the president's sense for rhyme, cadence to time the pauses, and alliteration that have remained in some of his most memorable expressions: "the fiery trail through which we pass," "the mystic chords of memory," "a house divided against itself cannot stand," or "the last full measure of devotion" to name but a few. Another significant example appears in his address of July 4, 1861, in "ballots are the rightful, and peaceful, successors of bullets." Lincoln knew that this antithesis and alliteration would leave an imprint on the listener.

Having experimented with the written and spoken word, Lincoln had recognized that "less is more." He had learned to avoid the flowery and ornate eloquence of his time that he had briefly embraced in his youth. Instead he tended toward short sentences and a compact style. He had a special talent for antithesis. In his Springfield Farewell address he expressed: "Without the assistance of that Divine Being . . . I cannot succeed. With that assistance I cannot fail." He used the negative as a basic rhetorical tool, or contrasted positive and negative actions or ends: "With malice towards none; with charity for all," "nobly save or meanly lose." To this Lincoln the

---

[87] Douglas L. Wilson, *Lincoln's Sword: The Presidency and the Power of Words*, 182.

writer added the use of the interrogatory mode and of probing questions, no doubt inherited from Lincoln the lawyer. The questions were often so formulated as to encapsulate a central dilemma, and support what would follow as answer.

The Most Important Speeches

Writing was such an important tool of Lincoln's presidency that he would not delegate it to others. And so important, as we have seen, that almost every word was weighed for its impact and implications. In addition, Lincoln clearly recognized the different impact and style in spoken and written word. He personally changed the wording of his spoken addresses when publishing them. Below are some of the most important speeches of his presidency, with an eye at their genesis, style, and intended effect.

The Message to Congress of July 4, 1861

By the time this speech was delivered, the Civil War was effectively on. Lincoln had to craft the message in such a way as to give Americans a feeling for what they were fighting for and a desire to engage in it. No doubt taking advantage of the speech's timing, he placed at the center of the address the right of free government by the people to protect and maintain itself. The viability of popular government was at stake in the active denying of a minority who sought power to dissolve what the majority had decided upon. He brought this issue beyond American borders; he turned it into an issue for humanity, as one of free government upon the earth and survival of democracy itself.

With this speech, Lincoln attempted at length to prove that the rebellion wanted to take advantage of rights it found in the Constitution to undermine the very nature of the Constitution and its existence. While he pointed out that the nation would be tested and this would require courage, he also acknowledged the exceptional circumstance of brother fighting brother in a civil war.

The message was generally well received. While the abolitionists were disappointed by the lack of reference to the slavery issue, the message served to reassure border states and the wavering Democrats that the central aim of the administration was the preservation of the Union.

The Seven Stages of the Message of July 4, 1861

Lincoln attributed great importance to his 4th of July, 4, 1861, Message to Congress. He started working on it by May of that year. Douglas L. Wilson recognizes seven stages to this process:

- Making notes: One example, the so-called Random 6 (name given by Lincoln), survives in the Library of Congress. This note highlights the importance of the contest, for the fate of democracy in the whole world, through reference to the threat to "put an end to free government upon the Earth."
- Preliminary drafts (none surviving).
- First handwritten draft (3,300 words): At this stage the president describes his personal involvement. He refers to himself, as in "I believed it would be utterly ruinous" and "I hesitated."
- Second handwritten draft (5,500 words): Incorporating the recommendations of his advisers, the "I" became "the executive" or "the administration." Self-reference or hesitation, in the preliminary draft, was changed to a more neutral "it was believed" or more resolute "this could not be allowed."
- First printed copy with revisions: Lincoln's editor John D. Defrees removed many of Lincoln's overabundant commas; Lincoln restored two of them and added five new ones in one page alone. He did not budge around the use of the word "sugar-coated" which Defrees objected to, and wanted to see replaced by "disguised" or "concealed." And he insisted on the use of the word "rebellion" in lieu of "secession."
- Second printed copy with revisions: At this stage Lincoln sought the advice of his secretary of state, William Seward. The latter recommended to soften the tone in places and to omit mention of the blockade of Southern harbors, because it stood at odds with international law. He also suggested a more careful use of the words "treason" and "traitors" for the effect this expression would have on border states citizens most of all. No reference to these survived. Treasonous became "injurious."
- Final version sent to Congress with revisions (6,400 words): This includes a new ending. The message would be silent on slavery, indicating that the president's goal was the preservation of the Union, not abolition, an important approach in reassuring border states and hesitant Democrats.

Source: Douglas, L. Wilson, *Lincoln's Sword: The Presidency and the Power of Words.*

The evolution of this Message to Congress can be followed in great detail (see box).

Emancipation Proclamation

Though Frederick Douglass called it "the greatest event of our nation's history" and Lincoln himself "the central act of my administration," this is a document that lags far behind all other most famous speeches in style and appeal. It is written in a very utilitarian style and in a pervasive legalistic tone. Its success, however, hinged upon these seemingly limiting constraints.

Consider that its immediate result was minimal, since it hardly freed any enslaved people. Rather, it kept them enslaved in large parts of the nation. Although personally averse to slavery, Lincoln was well aware that the rights of slaveholders were protected by the Constitution, and he accepted his lack of power in altering the matter. The proclamation was just a temporary war measure. In fact during the time leading to the speech, Lincoln had rescinded insubordinate Army officer orders freeing slaves.

The president understood slavery as a culturally inherited matter, and he did not want to qualify slaveholders as the evil to be fought against. He realized that had he been born in the South, he may have been one of them. More pragmatically he understood that abolitionism would never garner enough public support. Moreover, he knew that losing the four border states to the Confederacy practically meant losing the war!

Lincoln had been in anguish before issuing the proclamation. He had asked for the opinion of Gideon Welles and William Seward. Welles reported that on July 22, 1862, at a special session of his cabinet, the president announced, "The time has arrived when we must determine whether the slave element should be for or against us."[88] Lincoln, very much in doubt about the constitutionality of seizing rebel property, was still thinking in terms of compensation and possibly colonization. He was showing with these choices that he did not want to expropriate slaveholders. When he put this offer on the table, however, the border states refused compensated emancipation. Add to the above that emancipation was not widely popular in the North.

---

[88] Douglas L. Wilson, *Lincoln's Sword: The Presidency and the Power of Words*, 117.

The consultation with his cabinet members proved crucial to Lincoln. It was Seward who was instrumental in linking the passage of the proclamation to military victories, so as not to make it look like a desperate measure. And timing played once again a critical role in the president's moves.

In response to a public letter from Horace Greeley in the *New York Times*, "The Prayer of Twenty Millions" (August 20, 1862), lamenting the lack of action on the Second Confiscation Act, Lincoln wrote what became famous as his desire to save the Union, and how he would address it by freeing all or none of the slaves. The president had already decided to bring the issue in the open, and Horace Greeley's attack offered a perfect timing. The strategically minded president placed his reply in the *National Intelligencer*, pro-Union but antiemancipation.

In the final version of the proclamation, Lincoln brings forward the added element of the enlistment of ex-slaves, which at the time was a volatile issue. It was strategic as he felt it was vital to the survival of the Union, and the president felt he could add another small but bold step in the education of a nation.

The Gettysburg Address

Before the address people in the North were losing motivation to fight. They could no longer understand the purpose of the war. There had been staggering losses on both sides, even if the North had come out slightly ahead of the South. And there were calls for ending the war on compromise terms on the issue of slavery.

Lincoln had noticed the enduring central appeal of the idea of "equality of all men" as it was known from the Declaration of Independence, and could not fail to see how eminently absent it was from the Confederacy's statements. In fact, Alexander H. Stephens, vice-president of the Confederacy, had publicly denied the validity of the principle of equality of the Declaration of Independence thus: "In fact our new government is founded upon exactly the opposite idea . . . that the negro is not equal to the white man."[89]

With the providential great victories at Gettysburg and Vicksburg coming around the Fourth of July, the president risked an unplanned speech on the seventh, celebrating that the victories echoed what had been held true

---

[89] Douglas L. Wilson, *Lincoln's Sword: The Presidency and the Power of Words*, 207.

on an earlier Fourth of July. This explains why the president was willing to take considerable time away from Washington for such a seemingly inconspicuous event as the consecration of a memorial cemetery.

The address that resulted from his decision has been hailed for its eloquence and its brevity. It came as a real surprise after a two-hour speech. The advantage of such a concise statement was the ease of publication. Lincoln intended that it would be reprinted in its entirety in all prominent newspapers; he wanted to use it as an education piece.

As it turned out the address was even printed in Democratic papers. It was bound to kindle an emotive reaction in thousands of readers, in great part thanks to its eloquence, the style and rhythm of its sentences, and the opportune choice of words. Gettysburg was for Lincoln the opportunity to rekindle in the nation the words of the Declaration of Independence, the central idea from which he intended to build all other, related ones. He had managed to intertwine freedom and equality and their equal role in government by the people. The war to preserve the Union now became a war to preserve the principle of equality.

The address has become a celebrated writing in American literature, such are its nuances and literary techniques. Lincoln played with the sense of the word "dedicate," using it both in relation to the war cemetery and in relation to the ideals of the nation. Douglas L. Wilson calls the Gettysburg Address a prose poem, because it echoes what Emerson says about the power of a poem residing in "metre-making argument": "a thought so passionate and alive, that, like the spirit of a plant or an animal, it has an architecture of its own, and adorns nature with a new thing."[90]

The Gettysburg Address brought to consecration all of the efforts of Lincoln, ever since he fought against the repeal of the Missouri Compromise. Lincoln had not only refreshed American memory; he had also changed the way most Americans would come to see the "founding act." Author and historian Garry Wills commented that "Lincoln does not argue law or history, as Daniel Webster did. He *makes* history."[91]

---

[90] Douglas L. Wilson, *Lincoln's Sword: The Presidency and the Power of Words*, 236.

[91] Douglas L. Wilson, *Lincoln's Sword: The Presidency and the Power of Words*, 235.

Second Inaugural

At this point in his presidency, Lincoln's address reflected on the his effort to reach for a deeper understanding of the Civil War and the American soul. He wanted to understand it from the perspective of "God's will" and educate his fellow Americans about it, and thus see above partisan views of right and wrong. According to Herndon, Lincoln's views on divine will were as follows: "God starts causes, & effects follow those causes; & those Effects are at once, in the ages, causes as well as Effects—Hence the universal chain of causation."[92]

The view of God's justice became the centerpiece of the Second Inaugural. With this theme Lincoln showed that he was a completely practical man, able to deal with all logistical aspects of a protracted war, while at the same time deeply musing from a philosophical perspective at the meaning of world events. In the address he once again brought echoes of the references to the divine in the Declaration of Independence.

In a conciliatory spirit, but also wishing to honor historical truth, Lincoln attempts to show that the war was not the fault of the South, that there had been a deep complicity between South and North on the slavery issue. The above was expressed thus: "The prayers of both could not be answered— that of neither, has been answered fully." Furthermore to this he said, "He gives both north and south this terrible war as the woe due to those by whom the offense came." The address is filled with biblical spirit and ethos. Lincoln realizes that the war had been so long to wipe out the evil of two hundred and fifty years of slavery and the habits it had engendered, concluding that "the judgments of the Lord are true and righteous altogether." Lincoln may have known that he was taking the risk of assuming the mantle of a prophet. He did so because he was looking ahead at tempering the spirit of revenge. The ending comes in fact with a rousing appeal to forgiveness.

Lincoln greeted Frederick Douglass, who came to see him after the inauguration at the White House: "There is no man in the country whose opinion I value more than yours." And Douglass replied, "Mr. Lincoln, that [Second Inaugural] was a sacred effort."[93] Charles Francis Adams Jr., writing to his father, who had been Lincoln's minister to Great Britain, about the

---

[92] Douglas L. Wilson, *Lincoln's Sword: The Presidency and the Power of Words*, 251.
[93] Douglas L. Wilson, *Lincoln's Sword: The Presidency and the Power of Words*, 277.

inaugural has this to say: "This inaugural strikes me in its grand simplicity and directness as being for all time the historical keynote of this war; in it a people seemed to speak in the sublimely simple utterance of ruder times."[94] Naturally, the president decided to have the Inaugural speech printed for the press; once more the educational aspect was very consciously assumed.

Public Opinion

Lincoln was the consummate realist and diplomat. He knew that he couldn't lead with the Republicans alone; he needed the Democrats and the border states. And he understood that most were willing to fight for the preservation of the Union but not for the abolition of slavery. Repeatedly he would test ideas and see what could be the new frontiers that public opinion was willing to explore. To a gathering of Illinois Republicans he expressed it thus: "Our government rests in public opinion. Whoever can change public opinion, can change the government, practically just so much."[95]

Lincoln wanted to persuade and educate, and that is what he had done in his long career as a lawyer and as a political candidate. Being able to speak the language of the people, offering stories and humor to which people could relate, was a way to defuse opposition while calling on the sympathy and support of the electoral base.

By initially emphasizing one outcome, such as the Union's preservation, and deemphasizing another one, emancipation, Lincoln was able to strengthen the first in a way that would allow the other. He adopted the wisdom of Solon: "No more good must be attempted than the nation can bear." What he stated about the Emancipation Proclamation is profoundly revealing about his role as the nation's educator: "When I issued that proclamation, I was in great doubt about it myself. I did not think the people had been quite educated up to it."[96]

At the beginning of the war, the so-called Corning Letter, defending the suspension of habeas corpus, had been quite effective in generating understanding for Lincoln's choices. Through it he managed to defuse

---

94 Douglas L. Wilson, *Lincoln's Sword: The Presidency and the Power of Words*, 281.
95 Douglas L. Wilson, *Lincoln's Sword: The Presidency and the Power of Words*, 145.
96 Douglas L. Wilson, *Lincoln's Sword: The Presidency and the Power of Words*, 160.

concern for violation of civil liberties and to appease great part of the Democratic opposition.

Later in the conflict the Conkling letter carefully justified enlisting Black soldiers and doing so in a way that would win support. The letter appealed to reason, and addressed fears. It was very well received across the country. It was recognized that the president could get to the core of the matter and persuasively undermine opposing arguments.

Lincoln's writing earned growing praise. Harriet Beecher Stowe, who had met Lincoln at the White House, stated: "There are passages in his state papers that could not be better put; they are absolutely perfect. They are brief, condensed, intense, and with a power of insight and expression which makes them worthy to be inscribed in letters of gold."[97]

By 1864 people like George Templeton Strong came to realize Lincoln's role in promoting a national cultural revolution: "I think this great and blessed revolution is due, in no small degree, to A. Lincoln's sagacious policy." And further, "Unlike any other instance in our political annals, every letter he wrote, every speech he made, brought him nearer to the popular heart."[98] James M. McPherson echoed him in the essay "How Lincoln Won the War with Metaphors." In spite of his prophetic capacities, Emerson missed Lincoln's greatness until close to the end. However, in the eulogy he wrote, he recognized the greatness, not just of the man, but of his writings: "The weight and penetration of many passages in his letters, messages, and speeches, hidden now by the very closeness of their application to the moment, are destined hereafter to wide fame. What pregnant definitions; what unerring common sense; what foresight; and on great occasions, what lofty and more than natural, what humane tone!"

One could argue that Lincoln's words formed a fitting complement to the Romantic voices of Emerson, Thoreau, Hawthorne, Whitman, Alcott, and others.

---

[97] Douglas L. Wilson, *Lincoln's Sword: The Presidency and the Power of Words*, 196.
[98] Douglas L. Wilson, *Lincoln's Sword: The Presidency and the Power of Words*, 245.

Lincoln's Spirituality

How could a simple individual with little education in his upbringing affect so powerfully the fate of a nation? We have seen the far-reaching capacities of Lincoln as a lawyer, politician, orator, writer, and educator. Behind all of these stood Lincoln the moral figure, Lincoln whose perception of spiritual matters towered beyond anyone of his time in America, save the likes of the Transcendentalists. One would not normally expect such an individual to work within the halls of government.

Part of Lincoln's make-up and capacities was announced in his father and mother, though this would just be a pale shadow of things to come. Certain psychic capacities were present in either one of them. Thomas Lincoln had a recurring dream of the woman he would marry and how he would meet her, until the dream came true.[99] Lincoln affirmed similarities in relation to his mother: "Visions are not uncommon to me. Nor were they uncommon to that blessed mother of mine. . . . She often spoke of things that would happen [and] even foretold her early death . . . just when she would die."[100]

Lincoln's Psychic Abilities

Lincoln himself had a certain prescience of things to come. To his friend Joshua Speed he declared: "I always did have strong tendency to mysticism. . . . I have had so many evidences of God's direction, so many instances when I have been controlled by some other power than my own will, that I cannot doubt this power comes from above."[101] More specifically, to Ward Hill Lamon Lincoln claimed that "he did not recollect the time when he did not believe that he would at some day be a future president."[102]

Lincoln's abilities had matured under adversity. The mother had died when Lincoln was nine, his only brother while in infancy. His sister died in childbirth when he was eighteen, and Ann Rutledge in the middle of their

---

[99] Susan B. Martinez, *The Psychic Life of Abraham Lincoln*, 35.

[100] Lloyd Ostendorf and Walter Olesky, editors, *Lincoln's Unknown Private Life, an Oral History by His Black Housekeeper Mariah Vance, 1850–60*, 158, quoted in Susan B. Martinez, *The Psychic Life of Abraham Lincoln*, 35.

[101] Susan B. Martinez, *The Psychic Life of Abraham Lincoln*, 27.

[102] Susan B. Martinez, *The Psychic Life of Abraham Lincoln*, 38.

courtship, leaving Lincoln, twenty-six, in a state of almost suicidal despair. Additionally at age ten Lincoln suffered a horse's kick on his forehead. He laid unconscious until he was discovered, and survived without apparent permanent damage. One is left to wonder if some spiritual faculty was awakened from such an unusually intense experience.

Other small examples attest to Lincoln's psychic faculties. One night the president entered the War Department in panic, and asked the operator to get in touch with the Union commanders, because he was convinced that the Confederates were about to cut through Federal lines. When the operator asked how he knew that, he replied, "My God, man! I saw it," meaning in a dream. The operator checked that the information was true.[103]

Lincoln's spirituality was no doubt accelerated in facing the trials of the nation, the fragile mental health of his wife Mary Todd, and the tragic early deaths of his sons Eddie and Willie. This was a continuous trial by fire that tempered the man's resilience and deepened his spiritual temper.

Already in 1860 Lincoln had what we could call a doppelgänger experience. The story was retold by his bodyguard Ward Hill Lamon, his secretary John Hay, and Noah Brooks, a journalist and personal friend to the president:

> Opposite to where I lay was a bureau with a swinging glass upon it, and looking in that glass, I saw myself reflected nearly at full length, but my face, I noticed, had two separate and distinct images, the tip of the nose of one being about three inches from the tip of the other. I was a little bothered. . . . I noticed that one of the faces was paler—say, five shades—than the other. . . . I told my wife about it; she thought it was a sign that I was to be elected to a second term in office, and that the paleness was an omen that I should not see life through the second term. A few days after, I tried the experiment again, when sure enough, the thing came back again; but I never succeeded in bringing the ghost back after that.[104]

[103] Susan B. Martinez, *The Psychic Life of Abraham Lincoln*, 185.
[104] Susan B. Martinez, *The Psychic Life of Abraham Lincoln*, 75–77.

The experience was preceded by intense stress and great fatigue, which is a current condition for heautoscopy, or seeing one's body from a distance.

The premonition was reaffirmed in Lincoln's last dream. In it he first heard people sobbing, but the mourners were invisible. Then he arrived at the White House's East Room, he saw a catafalque on which rested a corpse. Upon asking who was resting there, he was told "the president."[105] Later he belittled the dream to assuage those around him. But he had spoken of his early death to others, such as Herndon, Ward Hill Lamon, and Harriet Beecher Stowe.[106]

After Willie's death, Lincoln was often seen with a Bible in his hand. He apparently devoted more of his attention to the reality of eternal life, and to the life of prayer. Mary Lincoln expressed to W. Herndon that she thought her husband had had a religious experience following Willie's death.[107] Sometime after Willie's departure, Lincoln started to have the feeling that Willie was around. To Chase he confided, "Ever since Willie's death, I catch myself involuntarily talking to him, as if he were with me, and I feel that he is."[108]

Lincoln's Christianity

Lincoln's natural perceptions were enhanced by a deep interest in matters of faith. Historian James Garfield Randall reflects the opinion of this author when he states, "Surely, among successful American politicians, Lincoln is unique in the way he breathed the spirit of Christ while disregarding the letter of Christian doctrine."[109] Historian Nathaniel Stephenson adds, "His religion continues to resist intellectual formulation."

In no unusual way for the time he lived in, the Bible was probably the only book that the Lincolns owned. His mother, Nancy Hanks, though most likely illiterate, could recite portions of it as she did her chores. Frontier preachers' sermons were Lincoln's introduction to public speaking; he loved to imitate their fire and brimstone style.

Lincoln soon acquired a sufficient grasp of the Bible to be able to write

---

[105] Susan B. Martinez, *The Psychic Life of Abraham Lincoln*, 229–230.

[106] Susan B. Martinez, *The Psychic Life of Abraham Lincoln*, 231.

[107] Susan B. Martinez, *The Psychic Life of Abraham Lincoln*, 119.

[108] Susan B. Martinez, *The Psychic Life of Abraham Lincoln*, 121.

[109] William J. Wolf, *Lincoln's Religion*, 192.

a parody of the stories of the patriarchs called *The Chronicles of Reuben* in which he mocked the Grigsby Brothers, his rivals. Only after his arrival at Springfield was Lincoln exposed to more intellectually sophisticated pastors, who would have access to and interest in the scientific knowledge of the time. His first inquiries evolved from reading Thomas Payne's *Age of Reason*, and Count of Volney's *Ruins of Empires*. These probably forged new insights and questions, and shaped his critical thinking capacities. Lincoln made it a point to be able to re-create inwardly all of their thinking.

As a result of the above, according to Herndon, "he prepared an extended essay—called by many, a book—in which he made an argument against Christianity, striving to prove that the Bible was not inspired, and therefore not God's revelation, and that Jesus Christ was not the son of God."[110] His employer took the book away from Lincoln and flung it into the stove. He wanted to preserve Lincoln's political future, since these were very charged topics for the time that could have led Lincoln's entourage to see him as a heretic of sorts. His political future could in effect have been compromised.[111]

It is interesting to note that these events may have been associated with a time of inner battle, as it seems confirmed by the witness of Mrs. Rankin, at whose house in Petersburg Lincoln occasionally stayed. She reported Lincoln's words taken down by her son:

> Those days of trouble found me tossed amid a sea of questionings. They piled upon me. . . . Through all I groped my way until I found a stronger and higher grasp of thought, one that reached beyond this life with a clearness and satisfaction I had never known before. The Scriptures unfolded before me with a deeper and more logical appeal, through these new experiences, than anything else I could find to turn to, or even before had found in them. I do not claim that all my doubts were removed then, or since that time have been swept away. They are not. . . . I doubt

---

[110] William J. Wolf, *The Almost Chosen People: A Study of the Religion of Abraham Lincoln*, 45.
[111] Susan B. Martinez, *The Psychic Life of Abraham Lincoln*, 47.

the possibility, or propriety, of settling the religion of Jesus
Christ in the models of man-made creeds and dogmas.[112]

It seems that an important maturation of an independent and completely
personal approach to Christianity was maturing in Lincoln's soul. The
tenor of what he stated in the following years certainly bears weight to this
experience.

The above transformation may have deepened at the death of Eddie
in 1850. At the time Lincoln read very carefully the 600-page book *The
Christian's Defense* by Reverend James Smith. He heartily related to the
author, who had been an unbeliever and had a deep knowledge of the works
of Payne and Volney, as well as others, whom he now refuted. Through
his work Lincoln further bridged the distance between reason and faith,
which is what the author attempted. The following was reported by Lincoln's
brother-in-law, Ninian W. Edwards: "I have been reading a work by Dr.
Smith on the evidences of Christianity, and have heard him preach and
converse on the subject and am now convinced of the truth of the Christian
religion." Lincoln went even further in attempting to reconcile scientific
and religious thinking by reading Robert Chambers's *Vestiges of the Natural
History of Creation*, whose successive, revised editions incorporated the
newest scientific discoveries. One of Lincoln's major interests lay in the
topic of evolution.[113]

Influence of Scriptures

No president has ever had a better grasp of the Bible than Lincoln. And no
one has made more direct or indirect references to it in his addresses and
papers. This happened even in things scientific such as his "First Lecture
on Discoveries and Inventions" of 1858, with many references to Genesis
and Exodus.[114] The Second Inaugural Address alone contains four direct
quotations from Genesis, Psalms, and Matthew, and other allusions to
scriptural teaching.

The president was so versed in Bible knowledge that he could rebut
scriptural quotes with his own quotes from the Bible. From what we saw

[112] William J. Wolf, *Lincoln's Religion*, 52.
[113] William J. Wolf, *Lincoln's Religion*, 86–87.
[114] William J. Wolf, *Lincoln's Religion*, 132.

above, Lincoln may have come to regard the Bible as a scientific work of a higher order, though this was most likely only an intuition.

Tokens of Lincoln's deference to the Bible appear here and there. In response to a gift of an ancient bound Bible, he said: "In regard to this great book, I have but to say, it is the best gift God has given to man. All the good Savior gave to the world was communicated through this book. But for it we could not know right from wrong. All things most desirable for man's welfare, here and hereafter, are to be found portrayed in it."[115]

Secretary of the Treasury L. E. Chittenden recorded in his *Recollections* what Lincoln communicated to him: "We have to believe many things that we do not comprehend. The Bible is the only one that claims to be God's book—to comprise his law—his history. It contains an immense amount of evidence of its authenticity. . . . Now, let us treat the Bible fairly. If we had a witness on the stand whose general story we knew was true, we would believe him when he asserted facts of which we had no other evidence. We ought to treat the Bible with equal fairness."[116] To Speed, a self-proclaimed skeptic, who found Lincoln reading the Bible, Lincoln commented, "You are wrong, Speed; take all this Book upon reason that you can, and the balance on faith, and you will live and die a happier and better person."[117]

Despite all of the above, Lincoln's Christianity was completely devoid of dogma. He claimed the Bible's authority over that of any denomination. His not being member of any denomination came at a political price.

In 1941 what appears to have been one of Lincoln's printed pamphlets was discovered. In it Lincoln defended his religious choices to protect his political career. Excerpts of it are very revealing of threads that continued lifelong: "That I am not a member of any Christian Church, is true; but I have never denied the truth of the Scriptures." To this he added, "It is true that in early life I was inclined to believe in what I understand is called the 'Doctrine of Necessity'—that is, that the human mind is impelled to action, or held in rest, by some power, over which the mind itself has no control."[118]

To Mrs. Rankin Lincoln expressed his reservations about denominational creeds. He added that he would only join a church that made Christ's law of

---

[115] William J. Wolf, *Lincoln's Religion*, 135.

[116] William J. Wolf, *Lincoln's Religion*, 136.

[117] William J. Wolf, *Lincoln's Religion*, 86.

[118] William J. Wolf, *The Almost Chosen People*, 73.

love to God and neighbor the sole condition of membership. Similarly, he avowed to Congressman Henry Deming in 1865, "When any church will inscribe over its altar as its sole qualification for membership the Savior's condensed statement of the substance of both the law and Gospel, Thou shalt love the Lord thy God with all thy heart, and with all thy soul, and with all thy mind, and thy neighbor as thyself—that Church will I join with all my heart and soul."[119] In the absence of that, the Bible remained Lincoln's ultimate authority.

The interest in the Bible as a source of truths and insights was accompanied with a prayer life that grew over the years and deepened Lincoln's "mysticism." To Rebecca Pomeroy, nurse to Willie and Tad, speaking to Lincoln about the prayers offered to him, Lincoln expressed his happiness at hearing the news and restated his need for support through prayer. On the occasion of the first inaugural, Mary Todd reported that Lincoln often retired and prayed audibly for strength and guidance. John Nicolay, his secretary, heard him say that he prayed, and that his prayer meant asking God to understand His purposes, rather than His granting of human wishes.

To General Sickles, who asked the president about his state of mind before the battle of Gettysburg, Lincoln replied:

> Well, I will tell you how it was. . . . Oppressed by the gravity of our affairs, I went to my room one day, and I locked the door, and got down on my knees before Almighty God, and prayed to Him mightily for victory at Gettysburg. . . . And I then and there made a solemn vow to Almighty God, that if He would stand by our boys at Gettysburg, I would stand by Him. And after that (I don't know how it was, and I can't explain it), soon a sweet comfort crept into my soul that God Almighty had taken the whole business into His own hands and that things would go all right at Gettysburg. And that is why I had no fears about you.[120]

And further, to his friend Noah Brooks he confided, "I have been driven

---

[119] William J. Wolf, *The Almost Chosen People*, 75.
[120] William J. Wolf, *The Almost Chosen People*, 125.

many times upon my knees by the overwhelming conviction that I had nowhere else to go."[121]

The examples given above could be multiplied by others. What is of greatest interest for spiritual seekers are Lincoln's fine balancing between faith and reason. To abolitionist clergy questioning him about abolition, Lincoln revealed his way of proceeding in balancing the requests of spirit and of reason: "Unless I am more deceived in myself than I often am, it is my earnest desire to know the will of Providence in this matter. And, if I can learn what it is, I will do it! These are not, however, the days of miracles, and I suppose it will be granted that I am not to expect direct revelation. I must study the plain, physical facts of the case, ascertain what is possible and learn what appears to be wise and right."[122] Interestingly this was said in early September 1862, when the president was thinking about the Emancipation Proclamation. In this, as in other matters, Lincoln was showing that prayer did not replace "cold, calculated, unimpassioned reason." It complemented it. Only after weighing at length the pros and cons did the president deliberate that there were more imponderables and that his reason could be illuminated by a higher perspective upon receiving guidance from the spirit. The spirit would affirm or rectify all the hard and necessary foot work.

Of all instances in which the above applies, the circumstances leading to the formulation of the Emancipation Proclamation and Lincoln's resolution to announce it are well documented. The president took a long time debating, envisioning, and then acting when the moment felt just right. Only when he could discern the will of God could he act with firmness. Fulfilling the will of God also meant affirming the decisions he had taken by virtue of his own judgment, only now made stronger, not denying self-responsibility.

Lincoln's Understanding of Christian Doctrine

Lincoln most often referred to Christ as "Savior" and "Lord." And he believed that His deed was ultimately meant for the redemption of all, which, arguably would have excluded him from any church of the time. Isaac Cogdal, with whom Lincoln talked on the matter in 1859, states that

---

[121] William J. Wolf, *The Almost Chosen People*, 125.
[122] William J. Wolf, *The Almost Chosen People*, 22.

"[Lincoln] understood punishment for sin to be a Bible doctrine; that the punishment was parental in its object, aim, and design, and intended for the good of the offender; hence it must cease when justice is satisfied."[123] The same is confirmed by Jonathan Harnett, a Lincoln associate and business man, regarding a conversation in Lincoln's office: "[Lincoln] left no room to doubt or question his soundness on the atonement of Christ, and salvation finally of all men. . . . The Saviour of all; and the supreme Ruler, he could not be with one out of the fold; all must come in with his understanding of the doctrine taught in the scriptures."[124]

All of the above explains both why Lincoln was deeply Christian, and why he could not belong to a church. His was a much wider, more encompassing view of Christianity, more reminiscent of Saint Paul's theology than of any denominational creed of his time. In light of all of this, it is not surprising to know that in his last carriage ride Lincoln had expressed to Mary that the city he most wanted to see was Jerusalem.[125]

In conjunction with his personal spiritual growth, Lincoln underwent a progressive understanding of the spiritual striving of the nation. It touched first on the matter of slavery, then on the understanding of its root economic causes that allied North and South in a deeper complicity. It finally led to an understanding of the reasons for the Civil War.

At the time of the Kansas-Nebraska Act, Lincoln came out of his political hibernation and started speaking against slavery from a biblical perspective, decrying that slaveholders were defying the injunction "in the sweat of thy face shall thou eat bread" while also doing so from the perspective of the Declaration of Independence's claim of the equality of all men. The reference to "the sweat of thy brow" returned in the Cincinnati speech of September 17, 1859: "As labor is the common burthen of our race, so the effort of some to shift their share of the burthen on to the shoulders of others, is the great, durable curse of the race. Originally a curse for transgression upon the whole race, when, as by slavery, it is concentrated on a party only, it becomes the double-refined curse of God upon His creatures." More and more Lincoln came to see slavery as a defiance of God's justice and contradiction of His

---

[123] William J. Wolf, *The Almost Chosen People*, 104.

[124] William J. Wolf, *Lincoln's Religion*, 106.

[125] Susan B. Martinez, *The Psychic Life of Abraham Lincoln*, 234.

will. Therefore he felt the nation was subject to God's judgment. And he understood that the judgment fell on both sides, since slavery was a national, not just a sectional evil.

Lincoln saw the Civil War as God's judgment meted out upon the nation for not putting slavery on the way of extinction, as many of the Founders had intended. The clinging to slavery was a "built-in contradiction to the law of its life."[126] This metaphysical view did not deny the historical, psychological, social, and political factors in the equation; it superseded all of them.

Lincoln conceived that the war would continue "until all the wealth piled by the bond-man's two hundred and fifty years of unrequited toil shall be sunk" (Second Inaugural Address). In parallel to his personal views of salvation, here too Lincoln saw this punishment as regenerative, intended for the renewal of an America further dedicated to the freedom of all its people.

The president could see the Civil War above the factions. In a letter to Albert Hodges, editor of the Frankfort (KY) *Commonwealth*, he stated, "If God wills the removal of a great wrong, and wills also that we of the North, as well as you of the South, shall pay fairly for our complicity in that wrong, impartial history will find therein new cause to attest and revere the justice and goodness of God."[127]

In Lincoln's views God guided human consciousness, so that their actions would be a response to His guidance. And He was overruling those deeds that were at cross-purposes with his guidance. America was in his perception "the almost chosen people." In Buffalo on the way to the White House he had said, "For the ability to perform it [his work as president] I must trust in that Supreme Being who has never forsaken this favored land, though the instrumentality of this great and intelligent people."[128]

Rededicating the Nation: A Transcendentalist President?

The above view of national matters highlights the coherence of initiatives taken during the years of conflict. At the end of July 1861, Lincoln appointed a national day of prayer and fasting, after the disaster of Bull Run. This was

[126] William J. Wolf, *Lincoln's Religion*, 25.
[127] William J. Wolf, *Lincoln's Religion*, 176.
[128] William J. Wolf, *Lincoln's Religion*, 117.

a call to recognize individual and national transgressions against the will of God. It said, among other things: "And whereas it is fit and becoming in all people, at all times, to acknowledge and revere the Supreme Government of God; to bow in humble submission to His chastisement; to confess and deplore their sins and transgression in the full conviction that the fear of the Lord is the beginning of wisdom . . . And whereas, when our beloved country, once, by the blessing of God, united, prosperous and happy, is now afflicted with faction and civil war, it is peculiarly fit for us to recognize the hand of God in this terrible visitation."[129] And a month after the Emancipation Proclamation, Lincoln called for Sabbath observance in the armed forces. In this he was referring to precedent, as his reference to General Washington made it clear.

At the suggestion of Senator Harlan of Iowa, asking a day for national prayer and humiliation, Lincoln again called for a national day of fasting and prayer on April 30, 1863. It read in part: "We have been preserved, these many years, in peace and prosperity. . . . But we have forgotten God. We have forgotten the gracious hand which preserved us in peace, and multiplied and enriched and strengthened us. . . . Intoxicated with unbroken success, we have become too self-sufficient to feel the necessity of redeeming and preserving grace, too proud to pray to the God that made us."[130] In the wake of the above steps, it was natural that the president should accept Sarah Hale's suggestion of a national Thanksgiving holiday. He did it in 1863, fixing the last Thursday of November date by proclamation, and legating the nation with an enduring and significant holiday.

At this point in his presidency, Lincoln wanted to reach for a deeper understanding of the Civil War and the American soul. He wanted to understand it from the perspective of "God's will" and educate his fellow Americans about it. He wanted to see above partisan views of right and wrong. This approach was already announced by Lincoln in his last debate with Douglas in Alton, where he took the high ground: "That is the issue that will continue in this country when these poor tongues of Judge Douglas and myself shall be silent. It is the eternal struggle between these two principles—right and wrong—throughout the world. They are two

---

[129] William J. Wolf, *Lincoln's Religion*, 121.
[130] William J. Wolf, *Lincoln's Religion*, 163.

principles that have stood face to face from the beginning of time; and will ever continue to struggle."

In concluding, it appears that Lincoln not only aimed at educating the nation toward a fuller understanding and implementation of its founding impulses. His aims stopped nothing short of spiritual regeneration. Lincoln was only entitled to accomplish this deed because his Christianity and spirituality were not those of any denomination or sect. They truly formed the more advanced, and at the same time more living, understanding of Christ that could be found in America at the time, if one excepts America's leading literary/philosophical authorities.

The young Lincoln seemed to be acting in his youthful education as one trying to recapture the seven liberal arts, dear to one of the School of Chartres. In his Lincoln incarnation, he reconstructed a bridge between reason and faith, much like Emerson, Thoreau, and all the American Transcendentalists. He used the pen and ideas much like they did. Had he not had to overcome an education deficit, and had he not identified with a political mission, we might remember him today as one of them.

What Steiner says of the most famous German Romantics also applies to the American Transcendentalists, their counterparts: "With them [the Romantics], thinking was entirely absorbed by poetic imagination."[131] Though writing official documents, Lincoln could not help but leave a deeply personal and artistic footprint. He could not help but speak through poetic imagination.

In Lincoln, as in the Transcendentalists or German Romantics, the soul is impelled to deny the prevalent materialistic worldview out of its inner strength. It wants to re-create the world out of itself through what Steiner called the "idea-experience" or "experienced idea." In Steiner's assessment, "In Goethe, Fichte and Schiller, the experienced idea—one could also say, the idea-experience—forces its way into the soul." It is this idea-experience that creates the solid ground for a worldview that sees the human being as perfect and as free as possible.[132]

Thanks to the inner confidence of the experienced idea, Lincoln could re-create a fuller understanding of Christian doctrine, dispensing with the

---

[131] Rudolf Steiner, *The Riddles of Philosophy*, Chapter 6: "The Age of Kant and Goethe."
[132] Rudolf Steiner, *The Riddles of Philosophy*, Chapter 6: "The Age of Kant and Goethe."

need for a particular creed. He effectively reached far beyond the contents of any given denomination.

What lived in the German Romantics or American Transcendentalists in thinking or feeling found a deeper rooting in the will in Lincoln. Time after time we see him impelled to find a place in politics out of an objective cultural call coming from the land, so to speak. It's as if Lincoln thought, "If we don't act now, everything that is best of the American founding impulse will be dead and buried." And to this he replied out of an instinctive elemental fashion, out of a deep inner connection forged by the coming Michaelic impulses that lived in him. He simply could not do otherwise.

Chapter 6

An America That Might Have Been: Lincoln and Reconstruction

LINCOLN'S VIEW OF RECONSTRUCTION WAS one of gradualism, moderation, and forgiveness. He believed in fact that this was "the greatest question ever presented to practical statesmanship."[133]

At the beginning of the conflict, Lincoln had sent troops to Maryland, Kentucky, and Missouri, and this had led to the reorganization of the governments of those states. In 1862 he had appointed military governors of Tennessee, Louisiana, Arkansas, and North Carolina. This was meant as a temporary measure to protect Unionists, including slaveholders, in order to reorganize and restore the states to the Union.

Conservative Republicans favored generous terms for the return of the South to the Union. The Radicals wanted to assure a radical reformation of economic and social life before the South could return to the Union; practically this meant treating it as a conquered nation. Lincoln remained carefully neutral amid rising tensions.

In the border states, compensated emancipation was Lincoln's cornerstone. He had offered it to Delaware as early as the fall of 1861. It failed, but it motivated Lincoln to extend bolder offers to all border states. The other approach, that of colonization, did not bode well. When it was offered to freed Black people in Washington D. C. in April 1862, no one took it up.

---

[133] David Herbert Donald, *Lincoln*, 467.

Lincoln offered gradual, compensated emancipation and colonization also to the seceded states. He probably did not expect them to agree with the plan, but wanted to give them every opportunity before issuing the Emancipation Proclamation. Meanwhile he continued to encourage Southern Unionists to hold congressional elections. And he let stand Attorney General Edward Bates's ruling that affirmed that freed slaves were American citizens, a decision that nullified the *Dred Scott* decision.

The Emancipation Proclamation did not abolish slavery as an institution. The possibility was left open for rebel states to seek readmission without abolishing slavery. And the Democrats seized on it in order to open negotiations with the Confederacy. Emancipation, Lincoln's opponents argued, was the chief obstacle to peace. Lincoln mounted a defense of his decision.

In response Lincoln issued in early December 1863 the Proclamation of Amnesty and Reconstruction, as part of his annual message. It was also known as the "10% plan" and it has been viewed as Lincoln's blueprint for Reconstruction. It precluded any negotiated settlement that contemplated the preservation of slavery. West Virginia approved a constitution in early 1863, becoming a state in June 1863 and completely abolishing slavery in early 1865. In Louisiana, where Lincoln was presented with contrasting proposals for the state's reconstruction, Lincoln endorsed the one that abolished slavery.

In the time that followed, Lincoln started defending the proclamation on the basis that the assistance and support of Black Americans were essential to the Union war effort, in order to continue to enlist their support to the Union cause. The object of the war had moved from the preservation to the Union to "a new birth of freedom."

Lincoln advanced the view that the Confederate states had never left the Union, over and against more radical interpretations that on the basis of their having left the Union, Congress could formulate and impose strict conditions for Reconstruction. The 10% plan guaranteed pardon to whosoever had participated in the rebellion, with restoration of all property, except for slaves, with the proviso that the person had to swear to uphold the Constitution and therefore accept emancipation. It was called the 10% plan because it required only 10% of the state's voters to take the oath in order to begin Reconstruction. The only ones excluded from pardon were high-ranking Confederate officers and those who had mistreated Union officers. There were no political or legal provisions concerning the rights of previously enslaved people.

There was a lot of doubt even among supporters about the wisdom of planning Reconstruction on such a low threshold as 10%. But Lincoln wanted to start small by inducing a small group within the seceded states to switch allegiances. And his plan was tempered by realism and mercy. The plan highlighted the difference between wartime emancipation and the deliberate abolition of slavery. It paved the way to constitutional abolition of slavery in the Republican platform.

The 10% plan facilitated the creation of new state governments. Louisiana (1864) and Arkansas (1864) drafted new constitutions abolishing slavery, which were recognized by Congress. Lincoln's long-term views can be measured by the fact that although border states Maryland and Missouri had refused compensated emancipation, they later abolished slavery on their own by early 1865.

Wartime Reconstruction and Reelection

The abolition of slavery had turned the timely restoration of the previous status quo all but impossible. This underscored the need for a constitutional amendment, the coming Thirteenth. Lincoln needed to be reelected in order to ensure his goals and political continuity. He pushed the amendment through the lame-duck session of the 38th Congress. It was adopted and submitted to the states for ratification.

Lincoln was willing to offer financial compensation for lost value of the formerly enslaved, as had been his policy all along. And he placed this estimate to as high as $400 million, which he believed Northerners would be willing to pay. In fact, Lincoln asked Congress for an appropriation of $400 million, half of which was to be paid by April 1, provided that the Thirteenth Amendment were ratified.

When the Thirteenth Amendment passed, Lincoln called the amendment "a king's cure for all the evils" since it addressed the precipitating cause of the war and eliminated the uncertainties associated with the Emancipation Proclamation. He called it "a great moral victory."

Congressional Republicans and Lincoln agreed on a bill establishing the Bureau of Refugees, Freedmen and Abandoned Lands (most often called "the Freedmen's Bureau"). Abandoned lands were to be made available for rental and sale in 40-acre plots to the formerly enslaved and loyal white refugees. This involved less than one million acres since Lincoln did not support land confiscation.

The Second Inaugural Address clearly linked the end of the war with reconciliation and forgiveness. Lincoln reminded Americans that they all bore guilt collectively for the sin of slavery. He wanted to balance mercy for the former Confederates with justice for the former slaves.

Lincoln's last speech on April 11, 1865, alluded to a coming announcement on Reconstruction that was never delivered. This was the first time that a president endorsed limited Black suffrage. Lincoln concluded that speech by pointing out that "no exclusive and inflexible plan" would be enforced on the seceded states, but specified that "important principles may, and must, be inflexible." He applauded Louisiana's new constitution that had authorized Black education as well as Black voting rights. In all of this Lincoln was adamant that the federal government was not to control the process of Reconstruction: "Their people must do that, though I reckon that at first some of them may do it badly."

Lincoln also approved Stanton's plan according to which there would be appointments of military governors for the seceded states until civilian governments would take over. Military authority would last while federal executive departments reestablished operations. Lincoln gave no indication of a precondition of Black suffrage as a term of readmission.

Lincoln and an America That Might Have Been

In his cycle *The Tales of Alvin Maker*, Orson Scott Card builds up an America that might have been. The climax is reached in the sixth, and last book, with the building of the interracial *Crystal City* on the shores of the Mississippi, and it is only natural that the figure of Lincoln enters in and plays a role at this time at the climax of the building of the city. Here is where he is first described:

"Old Abe? Well now, why didn't you say it was Old Abe from the start?"

"Old? The man I'm looking for can't be thirty yet."

"Well that's him, then. Tall and lanky, ugly as sin but sweet as sugar pie?

"I've heard rumors about his height," said Verily, "but the rest of your description awaits personal verification."

"Well he'll be in the general store, now that he's out of the store business himself. Or in Hiram's Tavern. But you know what? Just go out on the street and listen for laughter, follow the sound of it, and wherever it is coming from, there's Abe Lincoln, cause either he's causing the laughter or doing the laughing himself."

Lincoln was in the middle of a story. "So Coz says to me, Abe, isn't the front of the raft to supposed to point downriver? And I says to Coz, And so it is. And he says to me, No, Abe *that's* the front. And he pointed *up*stream, which made no sense at all. Well, now, that kind of illogic always riles me, not a lot, just a little, and I says, Now Coz, that was the front of the raft this morning, I agree, but wasn't it us decided which end of the raft was front? And therefore are we not entitled to change our minds and designate a new front, as circumstances change."

Now Verily hardly knew what the story was about, and he certainly did not know this Coz fellow Abe was talking about. But when the people in the store laughed— which they did about every six words on average—he couldn't help but join in. It wasn't just what Lincoln said, it was how he said it, such a dry manner, and willing to make himself the fool of the story, but a fool with sort of deeper wit about him.

What was most interesting to Verily, though, was the way Lincoln fit with the other folks in that room. There was not a soul there who had even the slightest friction between him and Lincoln. They all fit with him like a bosom friend. And yet he couldn't be best friends with every one of them. A man doesn't have time to make more than a couple of friends so close and dear that they don't envy you when you do well or scorn you when you do badly or become irritated with you for any number of little habits you have.

It went way beyond being likable. Verily had met a few who had something of a knack for that—you find them rather thick on the ground in the lawyering profession—and he found that no matter how good their knack was, when you weren't with them, you were really angry at being taken in, and even when you were in that spell, some of that anger remained with you. Verily would sense it, but it wasn't there. No, these people weren't being hoodwinked, and Lincoln wasn't doing it by some sort of hidden power. He was just telling stories, and they were enjoying both the tale and the teller."

Lincoln's Death

Many books have attempted to answer various questions about Lincoln's death circumstances and about the unanswered questions of the 1865 Conspiracy Trial, among which:

- Why was Lincoln not provided with adequate bodyguard protection on the night of his murder?
- Why was his only bodyguard absent during the murder and why was he not questioned?
- Was John Wilkes Booth (Lincoln's murderer) killed, or was it someone else, since numerous indications attest to Booth surviving the events by many decades?
- Why were eighteen pages missing from Booth's diary, which were only found later?

I will refer to David Balsiger and Charles E. Sellier Jr., *The Lincoln Conspiracy*, because this was compiled in 1977 and very well documented, thanks to access to Secret Service documents, congressmen's diaries, letters, manuscripts, deathbed confessions, and especially the missing pages of the diaries of Wilkes Booth, Lincoln's assassin.

Among the documents were the papers of Col. Lafayette C. Baker, chief of the National Detective Police; detective Andrew Potter Papers; Rep. George Julian Papers; War Secretary Edwin M. Stanton Papers, that include the missing John Wilkes Booth diary pages; and Booth's purported letter to the *National Intelligencer*, explaining why he intended to kill Lincoln. The eighteen missing Booth diary pages, mentioning the names (some of them coded) of seventy people directly, or indirectly, involved in the initial plan to kidnap Lincoln, were discovered by collector Joseph Lynch in 1974.[134]

Before Lincoln's reelection, Senator Judah Benjamin from Louisiana had arranged for Booth to meet in Richmond, Virginia, with prominent Northern speculators (from missing Booth diary pages). The speculators wanted to arrange for cotton to travel out of the Confederacy in exchange of meat imported therein that would support the Confederate Army.[135]

---

[134] David Balsiger and Charles E. Sellier Jr., *The Lincoln Conspiracy*, 11.
[135] David Balsiger and Charles E. Sellier Jr., *The Lincoln Conspiracy*, 58.

The blockade impeded the trade, save for some easement to the rules through the so-called cotton passes awarded to a small number of people, stipulating that the cotton had to be purchased with greenback dollars. But wartime seizures of rebel commodities by the National Detective Police, meat among them, prevented the deals from happening. At the reported meeting were bankers, industrialists, and politicians. Among these were Zachariah Chandler, a Radical Republican, and Senator John Conness; Samuel Noble, a cotton broker; and Thurlow Weed, a Washington banker.[136]

Not present was Ward Lamon, close to the president, who speculated heavily in cotton and gold. He was important because he had gained the trust of the president and could ask him to sign cotton passes. Much of the South's cotton had already passed through the hands of the speculators before the war. The meat and cash would have gone to Lee's army. And this is why Booth could support the plan in spite of dubious and questionable associations, like those of the speculators, whom he hated.

From Richmond, Booth went shortly after to Montreal where he met with a number of people. In his diary pages Booth mentions leaving an envelope with money at the home of Senator Benjamin Wade, the writer of the Wade-Davis Bill and chairman of the Committee on the Conduct of War, "one of the most belligerent men in Congress." This was the third Radical Booth had met, after Conness and Chandler at the Richmond meeting.[137]

At a still later date Booth met with Senator John Conness in Washington. At this point all of these steps were meant for a plan to kidnap the president, Vice-President Johnson, and Secretary of State Seward. In the event of success, the Radicals were planning to appoint an interim Radical Republican to run the executive and deny the moderate McClellan, whom they feared would have beaten Lincoln in November.[138] Stanton supported the Radicals' plans since the War Department would play a key role in the occupation of the South. He would yield influence over military governors and districts, and the same held true for the secret services of Colonel Baker, also involved in the plot. Stanton had major political ambitions, including running for the highest office. After Lincoln's reelection, the plans changed,

---

[136] David Balsiger and Charles E. Sellier Jr., *The Lincoln Conspiracy*, 59–60.

[137] David Balsiger and Charles E. Sellier Jr., *The Lincoln Conspiracy*, 64.

[138] David Balsiger and Charles E. Sellier Jr., *The Lincoln Conspiracy*, 69.

contemplating his assassination, though many of the same actors may have been involved in the later steps.

It seems many interests had rallied behind a concerted effort not to let Lincoln's views about Reconstruction prevail. Here too we can recognize a law, or obligation, that an initiate carries with him into succeeding earthly lives. Once he has taken interest in the development of his pupils, he is bound to support them in lives to come. We saw that example in Chapter 1 in relation to Giuseppe Garibaldi, Italy's liberator and Lincoln's contemporary. Having practically liberated most of Italy's territory, he a natural Republican, handed it on a plate to King Victor Emmanuel of the House of Savoy to retire in what was practically a deserted island.

Lincoln the president acted out of this old obligation, as did Garibaldi and Washington. He promoted the well-being of his cabinet members, even when these were working at cross-purposes with him. Lincoln no doubt saw through the forces that were aiming at undermining him, or even eliminating him. He nevertheless lived his life with little concern for those. He expressed himself thus in this regard: "If I am killed, I can die but once; but to live in constant dread of it, is to die over and over again."

Conclusions

IN HIS VISION AT VALLEY Forge, Washington had foreseen the challenges of times to come. It appeared in the prophetic images already mentioned in Chapter 1:

> And with this the dark, shadowy figure turned its face southward, and from Africa I saw an ill-omened specter approaching our land. It flitted slowly over every city and every town of the latter. The inhabitants presently set themselves in battle against each other. As I continued looking at the bright angel, on whose brow rested a crown of light on which was traced the word "Union," I saw the angel place an American flag between the divided nation, and say, "Remember, ye are brethren." Instantly, the inhabitants, casting from them their weapons, became friends once more, and united around the National Standard.

There is more than one link between George Washington and Abraham Lincoln in what we are about to explore. Like Washington, Lincoln saw himself as the tool for the aims of the spiritual world, something so demanding that he could fulfill only incompletely. Thus, in the highly symbolic grounds of Trenton, Lincoln said he hoped he could "be an humble instrument in the hands of the almighty, and of this, his almost chosen people, for perpetuating the object of that great struggle [that America embodied for the rest of the world."[139]

---

[139] Chicago speech of July 10, 1858.

Lincoln, Washington, and Franklin

Lincoln's inner world shaped his presidency and the conduct of the war, consequently also the nation. Here his words to a clergyman acquire particular depth: "If it were not for my firm belief in an over-ruling Providence, it would be difficult for me, in the midst of such complications of affairs, to keep my reason in its seat."[140] Lincoln's reason had supported his faith in his early days. Once he had acquired this grounding, it was faith that supported his reason at a time where trials oppressed him at the personal and national level.

At America's birth, two towering individuals had supported its birth pangs. During the time of the Civil War, Lincoln was mostly supported by the civil institutions that the forefathers had devised and implemented. No other individual came close to matching Lincoln's stature and sharing his burdens.

Lincoln and Washington

Lincoln has abundantly been seen as a second Washington. First among these is the judgment of poet and national moral authority Ralph Waldo Emerson: "Only Washington can compare with him." When Lincoln was reelected, another poet, Longfellow, cried, "The country will be saved!"

Lincoln foresaw that his responsibility in discharging his office would resemble those of Washington: Upon leaving Springfield for the capital, Lincoln declared, "I now leave, not knowing when, or whether ever, I may return with a task before me greater than that which rested upon Washington." Were it not for Lincoln's assured reputation for honesty and modesty, this could sound like an arrogant bravado.

Like Washington, Lincoln had all the physical and psychological endurance, stamina, and sheer willpower to face one challenge after the other without caving in to despair. Like the first president, he also knew how to work with what has been called and made famous as a "team of rivals" in his cabinet. The rivalries of Jefferson and Hamilton were present between Salmon Chase and William Seward or in Edwin Stanton. Each one of them, at different points in time, presented direct, challenging ambitions to the president himself.

Can we not sense in Lincoln an initiatic strength of a previous lifetime? This would be confirmed in the president's commitment to promote the well-being of each of his cabinet members and their harmonious collaboration. Even when

---

[140] Susan B. Martinez, *The Psychic Life of Abraham Lincoln*, 256.

collaboration came to an end, the president did not indulge in personal vendettas. Salmon Chase, whose resignation he had accepted, became the Supreme Court chief justice, in whose presence the president proffered the oath of office.

Like Washington, though not as directly, Lincoln was also the commander in chief on the military front. He did not operate on the front lines as did his predecessor. Nevertheless Lincoln was directly involved in selecting, choosing, promoting, or demoting the various generals and officers, until he could find a group of trusted initiative takers who made the resolution of the conflict possible.

In his time journalists had started to call Lincoln "the second Washington." His political adversary, then friend, William Seward acknowledged, "Providence had raised [Lincoln] up for this emergency, as signally as He raised up Washington for . . . our independence."[141] So did too Benjamin B. French in a poem he gave Mary Todd:

> "So Washington's and Lincoln's names
> Twined in a wreath shall be,
> One gave a Nation to the world
> The Other keeps it free."[142]

An inadvertent irony of fate brought the two individuals close: their birthdays, February 12 for Lincoln and February 22 for Washington. For a time, and/or varying according to places, Presidents' Day has come to be seen as the joint celebration of the two presidents. At any rate Lincoln's name is the one most closely associated with that of Washington. A hidden genius is at play here.[143]

Lincoln and Franklin

From other angles than the above, Lincoln's biography resembles much of the personality of Benjamin Franklin. The president held reason and dogma in balance in a way that was parallel to Benjamin Franklin. He saw them as

---

[141] Susan B. Martinez, *The Psychic Life of Abraham Lincoln*, 83.

[142] Susan B. Martinez, *The Psychic Life of Abraham Lincoln*, 83.

[143] From https://en.wikipedia.org/wiki/Washington's_Birthday: "The day is a state holiday in most states, with official names including Washington's Birthday, Presidents' Day, and Washington's and Lincoln's Birthday."

complementary, much as Franklin balanced science and humanism. Both Franklin's and Lincoln's faith were tested in personal ordeals. It was recorded by Mrs. Rankin at whose house in Petersburg Lincoln occasionally stayed. Franklin's inner turmoil, it is worth recalling, was resolved through a spiritual experience, the same in which his friend and benefactor, Thomas Denham, died.

Like Franklin, Lincoln had an uncanny understanding about the effects of alcohol. He believed that drinking muddles the mind, and it was natural for him to abstain. Lincoln felt alcohol made him feel "flabby and undone." He didn't smoke or chew tobacco, either. Yet he did not do so out of any self-righteous stance. He loved to tell the story of sharing a trip on the railroad with a friendly gentleman from Kentucky who offered him sequentially a plug of tobacco, a cigar, and a glass of brandy, but couldn't entice Lincoln with any of them. The Kentuckian told him, "See here, my jolly companion, I have gone through the world a great deal and have had much experience with men and women of all classes, and in all climes, and I have noticed one thing." What was it? "Those who have no vices have d—d few virtues." No doubt Franklin could have told a similar story.

Like his predecessor Lincoln could see the issues at stake with the long view. In one of many instances Lincoln stated, "The struggle of today is not altogether for today—it is for a vast future also. With a reliance on Providence, all the more firm and earnest, let us proceed in the great task which events have devolved upon us."[144] Like Franklin, Lincoln possessed long-term insights that he was willing to test and promote, while patiently waiting for the right time. Ruth Painter Randall, who wrote much about Mary Todd Lincoln, called him "a wizard and prophet. . . . He seems to have something of that prescience of the future, with which minds of the highest class are often gifted. . . . The prophet waits patiently for the coming events . . . and learns to labor and wait." Like Franklin, Lincoln used the weapon of humor to offer little pearls of wisdom and render them accessible educational tools (see box).

Lincoln had understood the role and nature of humor in the American soul. To Noah Brooks he offered, "The grim grotesqueness and extravagance of American humor [are] its most striking characteristics."[145] And he

---

[144] First State of the Union address (1861).

[145] Paul M. Zall, editor, *Abe Lincoln's Legacy of Laughter: Humorous Stories by and About Abraham Lincoln*, 36.

certainly matched the claims in many of his humorous offerings. Much of Lincoln's lesser-known quips address universal human matters, as had been the case in Franklin's *Poor Richard's Almanac*.

Lincoln's Quotable Wisdom

Just like Benjamin Franklin in his days, Lincoln has left us many quotable juicy bits of wisdom, some of which are familiar, though not necessarily remembered as his. Here are some:

"You can fool all the people some of the time, and some of the people all the time, but you cannot fool all the people all the time." [This is likely apocryphal; see https://web.archive.org/web/20210127031007/https://abrahamlincolnassociation.org/Newsletters/5-4.pdf]

"Leave nothing for tomorrow which can be done today."

"Better to remain silent and be thought a fool than to speak out and remove all doubt."

"Character is like a tree and reputation like a shadow. The shadow is what we think of it; the tree is the real thing."

"No man has a good enough memory to be a successful liar."

"He has a right to criticize, who has a heart to help."

"Most folks are about as happy as they make their minds up to be."

"A farce or comedy is best played; a tragedy is best read at home."

"I don't like that man. I must get to know him better."

"We can complain because rose bushes have thorns, or rejoice because thorn bushes have roses."

"My great concern is not whether you have failed, but whether you are content with your failure."

"Elections belong to the people. It's their decision. If they decide to turn their back on the fire and burn their behinds, then they will just have to sit on their blisters."

"In law it is a good policy to never plead what you need not, lest you oblige yourself to prove what you can not."

Franklin created the idea of America; he invited his fellow citizens to become something new and daring. Lincoln called America back to its founding impulse, in which lived much of Franklin's wisdom.

In summing up, Lincoln had both the overabundance of will forces that we recognized in George Washington, and the lightness, wisdom, and depth of insight that was displayed in his day by Benjamin Franklin. He can be said to have carried their mission further, in rising to the presidency 72 years after Washington.

The similarities between Lincoln and Franklin on one hand, Washington on the other, point to larger common circumstances that can escape a quick survey. Both the Revolutionary War and Civil War involved brothers fighting brothers. During the Revolutionary War, especially in the early stages, the population was divided between rebels and loyalists. When fighting broke out, a majority of English and British colonists found themselves fighting their counterparts from across the ocean.

In the times preceding the Revolutionary War, Franklin educated his fellow colonists to see themselves as Americans in a new nation. Washington embodied that ideal. He taught first his army, then the nation, what it meant to subordinate his personal capacities and ambitions to the Republican ideal, avoiding the temptations of personal power. His was an education in action. That process of education was continued in the formulation and ratification of the Constitution.

When Lincoln assumed power, an equal temptation lay open to him. He could have usurped powers in order to ensure the preservation of the Union; he could have enlarged the power of the executive at the expense of the legislative and judicial. Instead he maneuvered between each branch of power to negotiate, persuade, and preserve harmony. As we have illustrated in the previous chapters, he accomplished a great work of education in preserving the Republican ideal and persuading his fellow Americans that all human beings are really created equal.

Initiate of Old?

The life of the one whom they called "the Ancient One" was itself an initiation ordeal. He had to overcome humble beginnings, lack of education, the loss of many loved ones, repeated failure, and the nation's trial by fire in order to reawaken the capacities that lay dormant in his soul. What had met him as an initiation in a previous life reemerged as initiation through life, a trial by fire. His dormant capacities were thus reawakened.

In a talk that he had with the Treasury Secretary L. E. Chittenden, which the latter recorded, Lincoln delivers a testimonial of his living link to the spirit:

> That the almighty does make use of human agencies, and directly intervenes in human affairs, is one of the plainest statements in the Bible. I have had so many evidences of His direction, so many instances in which I have been controlled by some other power than my own will, that I cannot doubt that this power comes from above. I frequently see my way clear to a decision when I am conscious that I have no sufficient facts upon which to found it. But I cannot recall one instance in which I have followed my judgment, founded upon such a decision, when the results were unsatisfactory."[146]

This capacity of hearing in an inspired state is what others fathomed through direct observation of the president. An officer hearing the Gettysburg Address noticed that Lincoln, before beginning the address, looked as if his mind had been somewhere else, as if there had been a sort of otherworldliness in his demeanor.[147] Friends in Illinois had already noticed that Lincoln would seem at times as if in a world of his own, sitting in minutes of complete silence and gazing straight ahead. Other foreign visitors noticed that he could be in states of alternating consciousness. And a French visitor could count up to twenty such changes in an evening.[148] The painter Carpenter called these "his extraordinary moods of abstraction in which he was blind and deaf to all around him." To those unaware, this could look as if he were dozing off, or distracted.[149]

Herndon, who had been closer to Lincoln than many, noticed, "He can sit and think without food or rest longer than any man I ever saw." he also

[146] William J Wolf, *Lincoln's Religion*, 156.
[147] Susan B. Martinez, *The Psychic Life of Abraham Lincoln*, 191.
[148] Susan B. Martinez, *The Psychic Life of Abraham Lincoln*, 191.
[149] Susan B. Martinez, *The Psychic Life of Abraham Lincoln*, 192.

described him as "a peculiar man with a double consciousness, a double life. The two states, never in a normal man, co-exist in equal and vigorous activities though they succeed each other quickly."[150] Bad or sad news could trigger the almost disembodied state, even bring him to the place of nearly falling off his feet on few occasions, as upon receiving news of war defeats, like the news of Edward Baker's death at Red Bluff.

Lincoln, the African-American, and the Fate of America

The second half of the 19th century saw an important spiritual event influencing humanity: the fall of the spirits of darkness into the human/terrestrial realm following their battle with Michael. This started in the early 1840s and was completed by 1879, the watershed year of the new regency of Michael as time spirit. Among other aspects we can say that previous to that time, and ever since the time of the Fall, the progressive spirits had countered the spirits of darkness wanting to bestow independence to the individual who was not ready for it. This had been countered by the evolutionary spirits through placing the individual within the stream of heredity, within the blood bonds of tribes, nations, and races.

In preparation for the Michael Age, the individual now needs to affirm herself beyond blood ties; she needs to seek her spiritual belonging, no longer the ties of blood. In Steiner's words:

> [The year] 1841 saw the beginning of the mighty battle of which I have spoken. Then the spirits which are related to those others [the early regressive spirits] descended to join them below. The power of the old rebels, of the continuing stream of spirits of darkness who had their tasks to perform from Lemurian and Atlantean times, is gradually dying down as the powers of their brothers begin to take effect.

---

[150] Susan B. Martinez, *The Psychic Life of Abraham Lincoln*, 192.

Lincoln's Face

From a Scientific Perspective

"The left side of Lincoln's face was much smaller than the right, an aberration called cranial facial microsomia. The defect joins a long list of ailments—including smallpox, heart illness and depression—that modern doctors have diagnosed in Lincoln. . . . Most people's faces are asymmetrical, but Lincoln's case was extreme, with the bony ridge over his left eye rounder and thinner than the right side, and set backward." (Carla K. Johnson, The Associated Press, Aug. 13, 2007).

. . . and from an Artistic Perception

"It was not what he did or said that astonished me. It was what was in his face. . . . His posture is contained, his body seems to contain all that passes in his inward-directed face and eyes. And I see that it is Lincoln's body that gives his face such force. The face alone, yes, it is strong, perhaps even spiritual; but with the body, the relaxed body (a grown-up's relaxation, not a child's, not an animal's), everything in the face is rendered more objective; the qualities one feels in the face are verified, rendered part of nature, organic.

. . . In these old photographs, time is the photographer. Time always speaks the truth. And yet, in these photographs, Lincoln appears intensely individual, intensely alive and singular. This face is a face within which we sense the possibility and the right of a man to say I.

. . . That there should exist at the center of the American culture the ideal of such a man, such a human being, is not unusual in the history of nations and cultures. That this man should have been the most politically powerful man in the nation—that is remarkable. The central icon of our culture is a man of individual presence who is also immensely effective and engaged in all the outer forces of life—war, power, money, action, calculation, love and hate, negotiation, compromise—the whole world of the senses and the ego. The most powerful man in the United States and therefore, by then, already one of the most powerful men in the world: that this should have been a man of individual presence—that is remarkable. . . .

We can only say, with some degree of certainty, that his face calls us to the whole question of individuality as a conscious presence that transcends the ordinary meanings of the word "individualism."

The figure of Abraham Lincoln entirely eclipses this familiar dichotomy between individualism and social responsibility. . . . The face of Lincoln is not the face of a solitary or a recluse. Or should we say that yes, it is the face of a solitary who in his time was, paradoxically, perhaps the world's greatest and chief agent of action." (Excerpts from Jacob Needleman's "A Meditation on The Face of Lincoln," in *The American Soul*)

In more recent times, therefore, the spirits of light have changed their function. They now inspire human beings to develop independent ideas, feelings and impulses for freedom; they now make it their concern to establish the basis on which people can be independent individuals. And it is gradually becoming the task of the spirits who are related to the old spirits of darkness to work within the blood bonds.[151]

At the eve of the Civil War the matter of old blood ties had reached a fever pitch in the United States. The land that welcomed immigrants from many European nations, and had forced the immigration of Africans to its shores, was marked by a hardening of racial barriers. It was threatened by an impassable wall separating one race from the other. The institution of slavery, which had been blotted out from most parts of the world, was finding a haven and strengthening itself on American shores. The principle of equality of all human beings, so important to the new Michaelic Age, was threatened to its very core. Suffice to think what its repercussions would have been in a land that later welcomed immigrants from all continents, a land that has become a microcosm of the whole human race. How would that have been possible?

Lincoln's presidency served to repel all solutions that invalidated a Michaelic epilogue. It avoided the formation of a whole free nation alongside another one encoding slavery in all its institutions, which would have sought to expand to its south. It avoided all kinds of hybrid compromises making room for one degree of slavery or another. It returned America to its original impulse that recognized that all human beings are created equal, and extended the meaning of that equality.

To accomplish all of the above, Lincoln had to resist centrifugal forces that would have accepted a complete split, those that would have accepted a Union along very compromised principles and those that wanted to perpetuate the war by treating the South as an occupied nation.

Lincoln achieved an effective mediation between pro-slavery border states and Radicals and every force in between, such as the Democrats

---

[151] Rudolf Steiner, "The Spirits of Light and the Spirits of Darkness," Dornach, lecture of October 26, 1917.

seeking all sorts of early and fateful peace compromises. We could call the sixteenth president a radical moderate: radical in ideas, moderate in implementation. Far ahead of his fellow citizens in his views, he never felt he had the authority to impose them for expediency's sake, no matter how justified they could appear in hindsight. He helped and educated the nation to take the next steps only when it was ready. If in the end Lincoln achieved the goals of a Radical, in his demeanor and approach he was all but one. He did not want to import to the political process what is justified in the cultural realm. This highlights the relationship he had with Frederick Douglass. In effect, to someone who had lived slavery in his body, the steps taken by the president may have seemed exasperatingly slow.

When Lincoln issued the Emancipation Proclamation, it included a provision which called for the enlistment of Black soldiers in the Union Army. Douglass and other Black leaders joined the call for volunteers. However, Douglass was sour about the treatment of the Black soldiers and the discriminations that they suffered.

On August 1863 Douglass took an overnight train to Washington and sought an audience with the president the very same day. He had the good luck of meeting Senator Pomeroy, the antislavery senator of Kansas, who escorted him to Lincoln. Since Douglass had been critical of the president, he was also a little anxious about his reception. Lincoln treated him quite amiably, putting him at ease. But to the point of the retaliation to the excesses heaped up on Black soldiers in the South, Lincoln could only say that he was not comfortable with such a measure that inflicted a punishment on one person for a crime committed by someone else.

Douglass had to admit that "he saw the tender heart of the man rather than the stern warrior, . . . and while I could not agree with him, I could but respect his humane spirit." Lincoln agreed on principle on the idea of equal pay for white and Black people, and for the promotion of Black soldiers that the secretary of war would recommend. Douglass summed up his impressions of the president by saying that he was someone "whom I could love, honor and trust without reserve or doubt." Lincoln returned the compliment stating of Douglass that he was "one of the most meritorious men in America."[152]

---

[152] Russell Freedman, *Abraham Lincoln and Frederick Douglass: The Story Behind an American Friendship*, 84–85.

After the visit Douglass continued to be critical of Lincoln, in particular about the reticence to give the vote to Black people now that they had given their lives to the country. When he was invited again to the White House, Lincoln was worried about his prospects of reelection and had a plan to bring more enslaved people across Union lines into freedom. Douglass wanted to charge himself to organize a corps of scouts that would call for enslaved people to run across Union lines. He would have supplemented this idea by making emancipation the law of the land. Lincoln was enlisting Douglass to help him win the war, and Douglass needed Lincoln to bring a fatal blow to slavery. The abolitionist left the meeting more deeply convinced about Lincoln's moral opposition to slavery. The plan turned out to be unnecessary because of a series of victories of the Union Army, which also helped secure Lincoln's reelection.

Douglass finally threw his full support behind the president for his reelection. When that happened, Douglass wanted to congratulate him personally. He joined the celebrations of the inaugural reception at the White House, the first African American to do so. After gaining an audience he so much desired, he congratulated Lincoln about his inaugural speech.

This relationship is worth highlighting. Both Douglass and Lincoln were right from their own perspective; Lincoln in acting as a political figure, Douglass as a cultural/spiritual leader. In his writings Lincoln could inspire as a moral authority; in his position as politician, he was bound to other obligations. He could not act as a Radical, because that would have entailed forgetting his ultimate obligation toward the national compact that bound him to his office: the Constitution. Privately he had all the reasons to approve of Douglass, who could say all that the president couldn't.

Not only does Lincoln's life point to the past of the nation and the past of the Michaelic movement. He also shows the way forward to what America has to become. Echoes of the Civil War lived a hundred years later in the Civil Rights Movement, carrying further Lincoln's unfinished Reconstruction. Lincoln and Martin Luther King Jr both lived in a time of revolutionary ferment in the U.S. and in the world. Both worked in the '60s of their century, as Stephen B. Oates points out.[153] The Voting Rights Act that outlawed

---

[153] Stephen B. Oates, *Builders of the Dream: Abraham Lincoln and Martin Luther King, Jr.*

literacy tests and voting restrictions was the result of King's Selma campaign of 1965, one hundred years after the end of the Civil War.

King was an admirer of Lincoln and aware of the parallel themes of the Civil War and civil rights. The Emancipation Proclamation went into effect on January 1, 1863, and in 1963 King asked President Kennedy to offer a second Emancipation Proclamation. He later delivered his famous August 28, 1963, "I have a dream" speech at the Lincoln Memorial. King saw a new mission for the African American in introducing a new moral standard in the U.S. and in the world. Like Lincoln, King saw in the U.S. the land where the experiment of the integration of all races could take place. If it failed in America, it would equally fail the world over. King extended the message of Lincoln by seeing the dimension of globalization of world issues, and how America stood at the center of it all, for good or for ill.

Lincoln and the Future

We could argue that civil unrest is a constant American theme, a result of the emprise of the geographic double over the land. The present, extreme political polarization can be seen as a continuation of themes of previous centuries and millennia. It can indeed be linked to the centuries and millennia preceding the colonies.

The Maya superseded the decadent Olmecs at the time of Christ. A great spiritual confrontation pitted people of the same ethnicity against each other. The Maya, archaeologists agree, are of the same racial rootstock as the Olmecs. When the Aztecs rose to power, they certainly expanded their power over rival ethnic groups, but they equally subjugated and sacrificed members of their own groups. Continuous internal strife was part of their spiritual outlook.[154]

We will complete this exploration of America's sixteenth president with a look back to Washington and to the future of Lincoln's eternal individuality. That America has undergone other challenges after the Civil War is obvious; that it will soon undergo new ones seems unfortunately clear too. Those were already seen by George Washington, and they are worth quoting in

---

[154] These are themes the author treated in *Spiritual Turning Points of North American History*.

full. They form the last part of his vision at Valley Forge that we introduced in Chapter 1:

> Instantly a light as of a thousand suns shone down from above me, and pierced and broke into fragments the dark cloud which enveloped America. At the same moment the angel upon whose head still shone the word Union, and who bore our national flag in one hand and a sword in the other, descended from the heavens attended by legions of white spirits. These immediately joined the inhabitants of America, who I perceived were well-nigh overcome, but who immediately taking courage again, closed up their broken ranks and renewed the battle. Again, amid the fearful noise of the conflict, I heard the mysterious voice saying, "Son of the Republic, look and learn." As the voice ceased, the shadowy angel for the last time dipped water from the ocean and sprinkled it upon America. Instantly the dark cloud rolled back, together with the armies it had brought, leaving the inhabitants of the land victorious.
>
> Then once more I beheld the villages, towns and cities springing up where I had seen them before, while the bright angel, planting the azure standard he had brought in the midst of them, cried with a loud voice: "While the stars remain, and the heavens send down dew upon the earth, so long shall the Union last." And taking from his brow the crown on which blazoned the word "Union," he placed it upon the Standard while the people, kneeling down, said, "Amen."
>
> The scene instantly began to fade and dissolve, and I at last saw nothing but the rising, curling vapor I at first beheld. This also disappearing, I found myself once more gazing upon the mysterious visitor, who, in the same voice I had heard before, said, "Son of the Republic, what you have seen is thus interpreted: Three great perils will come upon the Republic. The most fearful is the third . . . passing which the whole world united shall not prevail against her.

Let every child of the Republic learn to live for his God, his land and Union." With these words the vision vanished, and I started from my seat and felt that I had seen a vision wherein had been shown to me the birth, progress, and destiny of the United States.

This, we could argue, is a danger of present or coming times.

As to what role the eternal individuality of Lincoln may play in future times, we will turn to another seer, the Russian Daniel Andreev, who spent ten years in the Russian gulags. Here he wrote his major work *The Rose Of The World* in which he details the coming of the future Antichrist in the person of the reincarnated Joseph Stalin. The vision that looked at Stalin's death makes reference to Lincoln thus: "In front of the walls of the Russian [subterranean demonic region] there unfolded [against the forces of darkness] one of the greatest battles of the forces of the Russian [saints and beings of Light] united with the Russian [folk spirit], and their forces proved to be insufficient. Angels rushed to help, also [many benevolent supernatural beings] and numerous other illuminated transcendental beings. For a while, one of the great illumined spirits was present there together with the [great company of] instreaming forces at the threshold of [the Russian subterranean demonic region] On Earth, this great spirit bore the name Abraham Lincoln."[155]

---

[155] Robert Powell, *Prophecy, Phenomena, Hope: The Real Meaning of 2012; Christ and the Maya Calendar*, 38. In brackets are some of the expressions used by Robert Powell to translate some of Andreev's unique expressions.

Bibliography

Balsiger, David, and Charles E. Sellier Jr., *The Lincoln Conspiracy* (Los Angeles: Schick Sunn Classic Books, 1977).

Calore, Paul, *The Causes of the Civil War: The Political, Cultural, Economic and Territorial Disputes between North and South* (Jefferson, NC: McFarland, 2008).

Dirck, Brian R., *Lincoln and the Constitution* (Carbondale, IL: Southern Illinois University Press, 2012).

Donald, David Herbert, *Lincoln* (New York: Simon and Schuster, 1995).

Emerson, Jason, *Lincoln the Inventor* (Carbondale, IL: Southern Illinois University Press, 2009).

Freedman, Russell, *Abraham Lincoln and Frederick Douglass: The Story Behind an American Friendship* (Boston: Clarion, 2012).

Freeman, Douglas Southall, *Washington: An Abridgment of the 7-Volume Opus* (New York: Touchstone, 1968).

Griffin, G. Edward, *The Creature from Jekyll Island: A Second Look at the Federal Reserve* (Appleton, WI: American Opinion, Second Edition, 1995).

Hodgson Brown, Ellen, *The Web of Debt: The Shocking Truth about Our Money System and How We Can Break Free* (Baton Rouge, LA: Third Millennium, third edition, 2010).

Holt, Michael F., *The Political Crisis of the 1850s* (New York: W. W. Norton, 1983).

Jefferson, Thomas, *The Writings of Thomas Jefferson: Being His Autobiography, Correspondence, Reports, Messages, Addresses, and Other Writings, Official and Private* (Washington, DC: Taylor and Maury, 1853)

Jennison, Keith W., *The Humorous Mr. Lincoln* (New York: Thomas Y. Crowell, 1965).

Keyserlingk, Johanna von, "Countess Keyserlingk on Spiritual Streams in the USA," *The Present Age* 4, no. 4 (July 2018), pp. 5–7.

Kolisko, Eugen, "Benjamin Franklin," *Shoreline, Journal for the Working Spirit*, November 1988.

Kotlarz, Richard, *The Iraq War and the Rest of the American Revolution: An Open Letter*, (2011), http://www.richardkotlarz.com/historical-events/.

Martinez, Susan B. *The Psychic Life of Abraham Lincoln*, (Franklin Lakes, NJ: Career Press, 2009).

McJimsey, George T., *The Dividing and Reuniting of America, 1848–1877*, second edition (Arlington Heights, IL: Forum, 1990).

Morelli, Luigi, *Legends and Stories for a Compassionate America* (Bloomington, IN: I-Universe, 2014).

Morelli, Luigi, *Spiritual Turning Points of North American History* (Great Barrington, MA: Lindisfarne, 2010).

Morris Jr., Roy, *The Long Pursuit: Abraham Lincoln's Thirty-Year Struggle with Stephen Douglas for the Heart and Soul of America* (New York: HarperCollins, 2008).

Oates, Stephen B., *Builders of the Dream: Abraham Lincoln and Martin Luther King, Jr.* (Fort Wayne, IN: Louis A. Warren, Lincoln Library and Museum, 1982).

Phillips, Donald T., *Lincoln on Leadership: Executive Strategies for Tough Times* (New York: Warner, 1993).

Powell, Robert, *Prophecy, Phenomena, Hope: The Real Meaning of 2012; Christ and the Maya Calendar* (Great Barrington, MA: Lindisfarne, 2011).

Rodrigue, John C., *Lincoln and Reconstruction* (Carbondale, IL: Southern Illinois University Press, 2013).

Steiner, Rudolf

- *The Riddles of Philosophy*, 1914
- *The Mystery of the Double: Geographic Medicine*, 1917
- *The Fall of the Spirits of Darkness*, 1917
- *Signs of the Times: Michael's War in Heaven and Its Reflection on the Earth*, 1918.
- *Color and the Human Races*, 1923.
- *The Book of Revelation and the Work of the Priest*, 1924.
- *Karmic Relationships*, volume 1, 1924.
- *Karmic Relationships*, Volume 3, 1924.
- *Karmic Relationships*, volume 7, 1924.

Swank, Walbrook D., *Old Abe's Jokes: Humorous Stories Told of and by Abraham Lincoln* (Shippensburg, PA: Burd Street, 1996).

Wilson, Douglas L., *Lincoln's Sword: The Presidency and the Power of Words* (New York: Vintage, 2007).

Woldman, Albert A., *Lawyer Lincoln* (New York: Carroll and Graf, 1936).

Wolf, William, J., *The Almost Chosen People: A Study of the Religion of Abraham Lincoln* (New York: Doubleday, 1959).

Wolf, William, J., *Lincoln's Religion* (Philadelphia: Pilgrim, 1970).

Wright, Esmond, *Franklin of Philadelphia* (Cambridge, MA: Belknap, 1986).

Wright, Esmond, editor, *Benjamin Franklin: His Life as He Wrote It* (London: Macmillan, 1962).

Zall, Paul M., editor, *Abe Lincoln's Legacy of Laughter: Humorous Stories by and About Abraham Lincoln* (Knoxville: University of Tennessee Press, 2007).

Internet Sources

https://www.blackpast.org/african-american- history/declaration-independence-and-debate-over-slavery/

https://wiki2.org/en/Slavery as a positive good in the United States

Printed in the United States
by Baker & Taylor Publisher Services